Praise for *The Hea*

"A very authentic and radiant book about the authors Mediumistic journey. Her explanation of the empathic, knowing child resonated with me deeply. She helped me to understand my own experience, ones I could not explain or define for myself until I met her. This is a must read for anyone who has experienced "knowing without knowing why". As an author and mentor, Deborah shares her path of self-awareness and Mediumistic gifts with each of us who longs for a better understanding of our own relationship with Spirit."

- Gabriela DeCicco, RN *and Medium*

"Deborah Finley is an amazing medium with a kind heart and an old soul. Her writing is a gift to those who want to understand what a true medium/psychic experiences. This book is a treasure for anyone who has had similar experiences or who knows a child who is sensitive. *The Compassionate Heart* shares important lessons sprinkled through with personal stories. It is as uplifting as it is informative. An easy, delightful read that I recommend to anyone interested in the truth about sensitives and mediums."

- Geralyn St. Joseph, author of *The Paranormal Activity series/Self-Empowerment series*

"A captivating narrative of Deborah's journey from being a Spiritually Sensitive child to her adult life as a practicing Evidential Spiritual Medium. The hurdles that she overcame and lessons that she learned are inspirational. If you are looking for a guide on your spiritual journey, you may well find them here."

– Larry L. Goble, *Jr. Reiki Master*

Praise for *The Heart of Compassion*

"This book chronicles Deb's journey as a natural medium - it gives you a peek into her empathic soul and allows a glimpse into the events that have shaped her into a talented medium full of heart and compassion. A combination of heartfelt stories and useful mediumistic information, Deb's honesty and candidness hooks you in with the first sentence and keeps you enthralled throughout!"

– Faith Chermak, *Paranormal Investigator*

"Deborah Finley's book is a fascinating bird's eye view of her self-discovery as an empath and medium. She takes you along for the ride as she grows from sensitive child into trusting her gifts. An interesting read for anyone wishing to open up their own intuition."

- Alex Daughety, *Empath and Intuitive Artist*

"Deborah Finley writes from a pure and compassionate heart. Her mediumistic experiences as a child, and later as an adult, has made me feel I wasn't alone in what I've felt and experienced as I learned to embrace my abilities. Deborah writes as if she is sitting across the table from you, drinking coffee or tea, teaching about spiritual truths in a down to earth way. I highly recommend this book!"

– Debra Brennan, *Intuitive Psychic and Professional Tarot and Rune Reader.*

The Heart of Compassion

A Medium's Journey

Deborah Finley

Powerful Potential and Purpose Publishing

The Heart of Compassion: A Medium's Journey
First published by Powerful Potential & Purpose Publishing 2020

First printing, September 2020

Cover art, graphics and book design by Candy Lyn Thomen - www.CandyLynCreates.com

ISBN: 978-1-7349655-4-4

Published in USA

Powerful
Potential and Purpose
PUBLISHING
www.PPP-Publishing.com
Hickory, NC - USA

This book is dedicated to my mother whose gifts
I inherited.

*I could not have asked for a better mother than you.
Knowing I am always loved is priceless and this is just one
of the many gifts you have given me. You are one of the
kindest, most intelligent women I know. Your wisdom and
strength amaze me. I love you Mom.*

"Our sorrow and wounds
are healed only when
we touch them with compassion."
– Buddha

Contents

Foreword

Our memories are the imprints of experience. As so often happens, they fade except for a few that stand out. In *The Heart of Compassion* we find a recollection of many unexpected accounts in the life of a natural medium. Whether a medium or not, they serve to remind that our own experiences have meaning and indeed lead us to places that we could have never gone in life without them. We are given a glimpse into the beauty and depth of the Great Mystery within ourselves and the Universe.

If you have ever had questions about what was behind some of your life experiences and wonder what would happen if you followed your inner knowing and passion, you will find this book to be inspiring. Through it, you may recognize the communication and connection with Spirit that has been present with you all along.

The Heart of Compassion is written from a first-person vantage point. I felt as if the author was sitting across the table, keeping me enthralled as the book unfolded. She lays bare the fears that are common to many of us in this area and as human beings confronted with things we do not understand. Overcoming these challenges, the excitement, and the rewards of following inner guidance are a powerful part of this telling as well.

Having read many fine books on this and related subjects and studied with some of the world's best teachers, this book is still captivating. Why? It provides a unique look through the eyes of an extraordinary human being and natural medium with a compassionate heart. Through those eyes, deeper insight into life's journey can be seen.

As you follow your compassionate heart and

further your journey with Spirit, allow yourself to set aside expectations for now. Liberate yourself from imprints of loss and fear to acknowledge the support, love and help that is all around you.

Marya OMalley, D.C., M.A.

Author of *You Are Simply Divine, A Handbook of Simple Spiritual Practices for Divine Connectivity and Divine Alignment Toolkit*

GRATITUDE AND THANKS

Thank you to my husband, who, after all these years remains the love of my life. Thanks for seeing the value in loving and supporting me in manifesting the dreams that are important to me. Thank you for literally building me walls. I will always love you, my always and forever man.

Thank you to my children, who are my heart. I am so blessed to have you both in my life. Your belief and love in me have always inspired me to be the best I can be. I thank God every day for you both, and I am forever grateful for you both. I love you to the moon and back and then some.

To all my family and friends. Thank you for your understanding during the process of writing my previous co-authored and current book. Thank you for still being there for me even after I ghosted you all!

Much love and light to you and yours.

ACKNOWLEDGEMENTS

I am grateful to my friend and colleague Gloria Coppola, for the opportunity to be one of her authors. *Surrendering to the Divine Plan* was my first story published in our co-authored, bestselling book, **Women Standing Strong Together**. Secondly, a channeled message from the Angels, *Messages from the Angels, Pathway to Awakening*, was published in the co-authored, bestselling book, **The Path of Awakening, A Healing Journey**.

Thank you for sharing your gifts of intuition with me, your intuitive coaching, and for the inspiration to write, which subsequently helped me to finally heal. You are a true wise one and healer.

I would like to acknowledge my administrative assistant, Deborah Lewen Myers, who is also an upcoming gifted Psychic Medium. Thank you for helping to recover files after an untimely computer crash in order to meet deadlines. Thank you for your honest feedback, unwavering patience, intelligence, and programming skills. Your grammar, and sentences structuring abilities are priceless as is your friendship.

I also thank my friend and colleague, Marya OMalley.

This has all been such an adventure. Through this experience I have received so many gifts, I have to pinch myself to make sure this is not all a dream!

Note from the Publisher and Editor:

The writing style in this book is in the first person, in the words of the author, keeping her personal language and vernacular intact to give you a more intimate sense of speaking directly with her. The channeled messages later in the book are also kept in the vernacular in which they were received.

"It is love that unites everything."

- Amma

Introduction

THE BEGINNING

In the Creator's intelligence, our lives are divinely orchestrated in so many ways that are far beyond humanity's ability to comprehend. In the midst of this divine order, God has a sense of humor. I didn't get it at first – just like some jokes – but I do now.

I write about many of the magical, and sometimes seemingly outright crazy experiences that are examples and excerpts from my life. My intention and hope by sharing is to inspire and educate you on many different levels. Some of you will recognize yourself. Others may come to understand their lives better. Still others may not feel so alone.

NATURAL MEDIUM

I am what is commonly known as a natural medium. You may be asking, "What is a natural medium?" It is a term used for someone who is born knowing with an awareness of the Spirit world. Interacting with the spirit world is just as natural to a medium as breathing is to you. As children this is something we do not question or even think about. We experience these interactions from the beginning of our life here. Most times I did not discuss what was so natural to me. If I was questioned, I answered honestly and to the best of my ability. It was normal for me to have my ancestors guide me from the spirit world since the very beginning of my life.

Even though I was taught manners and raised well, when it came to something I knew, because I felt it, I shared it. I was one of those children who had no filter and would just blurt out what came to me. You may be thinking most children have no filters and are honest, sometimes to a fault. This is true. The fact is I was reacting to something I was experiencing and did not fully understand. Consequently, my reaction to these experiences ended up creating a healthy dialogue between myself, parents, and grandparents.

My life has been filled with many interactions from Spirit, the Angels and Guides. I cannot remember a time when I did not hear Spirit, or my guide. By surrendering and trusting fully in that guidance, I have learned to walk through those doors, done the work, and have been rewarded on so many levels. Being of service to those in the afterlife is priceless. Being instrumental in helping their loved ones heal, or move along in their process of grief, fills my heart with gratitude.

These experiences with Spirit and our Guides continue to evolve and change, as we do, in order for us to grow. Natural mediums are provided the essential lessons so we can be of service to others, even though we do not know it at the time. This is what I meant when I say our Creator has an intelligence far beyond our human capacity of understanding, a purpose I will come to understand.

REVEALED INSIGHTS

All the memories of my life which were wiped out after having a near death experience were restored. There is no medical explanation for why this happened. The only explanation is that Spirit was preparing the way for me to write and heal.

Writing this book has healed me on so many levels. I hope this book gives you a sense of peace too as writing it has for me. In my role as a mentor, I have learned the value in sharing my experiences of how I grew and evolved into a professionally trained, schooled, and practicing Evidential Spiritual Medium.

Up until now, the things I share have remained private. By revealing these insights to you, I offer you an opportunity to have a better understanding of a medium's mind, compassionate heart, and the healing aspects of mediumship.

LEARNING THROUGH EXPERIENCE

I am not claiming to be a medical specialist or a neuroscientist. What I share within these pages are my personal experiences and what I have come to learn. The heart of the medium and the mind of the medium is like no other. Mediums see and think as well as process information differently. Trying to explain how our minds work does not always turn out well for fear of being judged. I have heard myself trying to explain to non-mediums how this gift works. I know how it sounds to some of them, because being empathic, I feel their feelings as well.

There is not a constant "buzzing of voices" going on in my mind. Thank God! Mediumship aside, I am like many of you. I am a wife, mother, and career woman. I am a multifaceted spiritual being having a human experience.

Years of searching for ways to better understand myself has led me to discover so much. The first thing I learned is I cannot continue to live my life pretending not to have these abilities or experiences. I came to understand people who are born with Mediumistic abilities tend to have many unusual experiences throughout their lives. Many experience traumas and close calls in different ways. Some work in fields where they are exposed to life and death experiences as well.

Knowing what I know now, if I were to take an educated guess, I would say this is to enable us to become better mediums. Through this we are able to serve our communities at a higher level.

I have the ability to revisit a period in my life, by focusing and moving my mind to that time. This is done through thought and intention. My mind goes backward in time searching, much like flipping through a Rolodex or flipping backward through a slide show of pictures. When my mind stops, I am the observer. God knows it took me long enough to finally stop running from myself long enough to deal with it all. However, the timing was perfect for me. By writing my story, I was given another example of insight and understanding of the power and intelligence of our Creator.

This book will take you on a journey. It is multifaceted and you will read about the in-betweens of my life, including how I came to understand myself and embraced being a medium. You will discover what it was like for me to be a natural medium as a child, a teen and then as an adult. I will share parts of myself and things never shared with anyone until now, you the reader. I will also share how I learned to grow and evolve.

I offer up little pieces of mentoring throughout my story with the intention of educating others and the hope of being able to help in some way, even to open minds to the possibilities of living life awakened.

When you finish reading this book, I hope you are as amazed as I am with the power of Spirit and begin to understand the magnitude of Intelligence behind our very existence. Perfectly orchestrating all our lives.

"Spiritual signs are all around you.
Open your heart and your soul to
believe as well as receive."
– Cath B Akesson

Part One

The Gifted Child

Everything you want to know
is already within you.
– James Van Praagh

A Sensitive and the Warnings

A SENSITIVE

I would like to introduce you to the sensitive child and how their empathetic hearts bring much empathy and compassion to those grieving the loss of their loved ones. In this story, you will learn through my experiences growing up as a natural psychic and mediumistic empath, how to help your child and perhaps understand your own journey more fully.

As a sensitive, your child will feel things more deeply than others who are not empathic. These children have been described as hypersensitive, melodramatic, or too emotional. This is not to say they are not strong, because they are incredibly strong and surprisingly optimistic. The empathic child is the one who walks up to the sad parent with tears in their own eyes. It is the child whose heart opens with compassion, upon seeing their mother suffering with a migraine headache and makes the wish for their mommy to have the headache go away. They are the beings born with a compassionate heart.

A child will blame themselves or sometimes internalize feelings of guilt for things that go wrong around them. The likelihood of this increases with a psychic child. Imagine if your child sensed things that were going to happen before it really happened. They tend to feel responsible when the responsibility was not theirs to begin with. If you are a parent of a sensitive, the likelihood this will happen is even greater.

The memory of the first time I knew someone was going to die seemed to come out of nowhere. Not knowing what to do with this information, I did not tell them they were going to die. When they died, I remembered thinking I should have told them. I thought maybe they could go to a doctor to get fixed. I will be sharing this story and many more so you can understand this gift and the challenges it presents for children.

It is important to keep an open dialogue with your sensitive child. Help them explore and understand their abilities. Focusing on the positives will also help them flourish. While keeping their age and maturity levels in mind, ask them questions about what they are experiencing. Help them to understand as much as possible. Kindness and honesty are key and will be important to them throughout their lives. Always love them for who they are without judgement.

THE WARNINGS

I was walking home from church one day, wishing I had listened to my mother about which coat to wear. Being a teenage girl at the time, I was excited about wearing my new 'chubby' jacket. I did not listen to her when she told me it was supposed to get colder and extremely windy later in the day.

The streets were empty. I remember thinking at the time it felt almost eerie. The wind was like a whip as it blew unmercifully, cutting into my bare cheeks. I was glad I was almost home. I was imagining myself making a cup of hot cocoa when my attention was drawn to a beige Volkswagen heading towards me. *That is cool,* I thought. My Nan used to have the same kind of car, right down to its color. As the car drove past, the man who was driving was looking at me. Our eyes locked briefly. For some reason, the way he looked at me made me feel like I needed to run. I had a strong inner sense telling me, '*Don't show any of the fear*' which was rising in me. *Stay calm, do not run,* I thought.

I became aware I could hear the motor getting louder when it should have been fading into the distance. *He must have turned the car around,* I thought. By this time, I walked faster and noticed the car was now slowly following me. *Do not show fear, just keep pretending I was not on to him.*

The chill which ran through me to the bones was not from the icy wind. Instantly I had a knowing, a sense he was dangerous. I thought, *do not go home,* because he would then know where I lived. I could see my street just ahead. I was so close to my house. "Do not go home," I clearly heard inside of my head. God how I wished I had just stayed home!

Crossing the street, I nonchalantly turned left, walking down the street before mine, instead of continuing straight ahead. The car also turned. As I sped up my pace, so did he. I began to run. I could feel his excitement rising. Again, I crossed the street pretending I was going to walk straight. The man drove past me, heading towards the park. He stopped at the stop sign. His car was a good bit ahead of me. I started backtracking, turning right, running down a different street. As I ran, I was praying my friends were home. Glancing back over my shoulder, I felt relieved thinking the car continued to go straight.

Still not taking any chances, I reached their house and began to franticly knock on their door. No answer. My mind began to fill with panic. Thinking, *Oh my God, please somebody be home!* I looked into their window hoping to see someone there. As I walked out onto their front lawn, I thought I had heard someone yell something from above me. I looked upward in the direction the voice came from, only to see the gray, cloudy sky. Then I heard it again, only louder, "DEBBIE, WATCH OUT!" This was clear as a bell. Hope and relief filled me as I scanned the upstairs windows thinking someone must have hollered from one of them. No one was there. I was confused for a moment. I thought for sure someone had yelled to me from an upstairs window. Then from behind me, I clearly heard, "He is going to get you. Watch out! RUN! He is behind you!" I turned towards the voice. Time seemed to stand still; the man was sneaking up on me! I was like a deer caught in the headlights as I looked at him. He paused for a moment, appearing to enjoy how fearful I was.

All the backyards were fenced in and he was getting too close. I was trapped with nowhere to run. As I watched him move towards me, the look on his face was one I had never seen before but knew it to be dangerous and EVIL. Terror ran through me all the way to my bones. I screamed bloody murder, as I heard the voice in my mind, *"Do not go towards him, do not! You can and will get away, do not give up, jump the fences."*

Screaming, I ran and jumped the fence. Once on the other side, I briefly glanced backwards to see if he followed. I was making too much noise, which made him hesitate, as he looked around to see if anyone was alerted. At first, he started to follow me. I had already put a fence and too much distance between us. He looked back at his car for a moment and I noticed the car door was opened. He headed to his car again. By that time, I was jumping the back fence into another back yard. Thankfully, there were no ferocious dogs in my path. My legs felt weak. I was breathing hard, gasping for air. *Keep going*, I thought. I found myself gulping huge amounts of air in, then holding it before letting it out. In my mind I heard, "*You are going to be alright, I promise. Just listen to me.*" I reached a front fence, jumped over it, and ran towards the street.

Normally, I loved all the open space where I grew up, but not today. The average back yard was at least a half to one acre long. I always had trouble running and would get winded quickly. The cold wind was burning my lungs, my cheeks felt like they were on fire and felt hot to my touch.

I stopped briefly, looking for signs of people. I contemplated cutting through the yards again to my street but changed my mind. I thought he might already be there waiting for me. With this thought in mind, I ran towards the bottom of the street. Yes! To my left, someone had their screen door open. I screamed again, running towards the door. *Oh shit, damn it!* The man turned onto the street and blocked my path to safety. "Somebody please help me!" I screamed to the opened door across the street. *You cannot make it*, I thought, as I gave the door one last look. Thinking to myself, *if I give up now, there was no doubt he was going to rape, torture, and kill me.* He was calmly enjoying this game of cat and mouse.

Just run partly back up the street, I thought, running as quickly as possible. My legs felt like they were going to buckle out from beneath me. Determined, I continued to run up the street. The man followed in his car, just as I hoped he would. My house was only another two backyards and one street away. I looked at the yards, there were no fences, only huge hills. My legs were burning with fatigue. I knew I would not be able to outrun him.

Without any warning, I changed directions once again. I was screaming like a mad woman, running straight towards his car. I could see him getting ready to open the door, his energy was creeping me out. His evil face smirking with anticipation. The car door was opening. Instead of going straight, I darted across the front of his car, making it to the other side of the street. All the while, still screaming at the top of my lungs, not daring to look behind me as I reached for the opened screen door I was trying to get to earlier. Finding the door unlocked (and yes, despite the desperate moment, I remembered my manners!) I banged on it loudly. I sneaked a quick look back at the car, saw the man just standing there, with one foot inside the car, preparing to get back in if needed.

I think he was waiting to see if a woman came to the door. I did not want anyone to get hurt because of me. I stood at the door, screaming at the top of my lungs, "Help!!! There is a man chasing me, someone help me!!!"

"Open the door and get inside," I heard the voice in my mind say. I opened the door, stepped inside, and locked the storm door behind me. I was shaking all over, gasping, and sobbing all at once. My voice was hoarse. The man's car was still there, watching and waiting. I shut and locked the main door.

Call the police, my mind thought.

Behind me I heard a voice angrily ask "What are you doing?"

HELP IN A BATHROBE

I turned around and there stood, not a woman, but a man! The man looked to be approximately the same height and build as my father. He had curly white hair. I began to apologize, and noticed he was standing there in his underwear, his bathrobe opened. He looked incredibly angry. Briefly, I wondered if the other man had led me into a trap? "Oh, dear God, help me!" I blurted out, beginning to panic once more.

Seeing the fear in my eyes, he quickly closed his robe, reassured me, "Pardon me, I am not going to hurt you!" I heard my inner voice tell me not to worry, I was safe for now. I stopped screaming and asked the man for help. "Where is he? I heard you screaming, and I was on my way to see what was going on!" he explained.

I pointed to the door. "He is out there!" The man's face grew angry again. He unlocked the doors and stepped outside. Fearing for this man's safety, I fought the panic rising inside of me. Seeing the car the man said, "There he is!" and walked down the steps, heading towards the car. I followed.

"No!" I screamed, begging, "Please, what if he kills you?"

Suddenly, a foggy patch behind the other man's car seemed to be building, rolling towards us like clouds moving across the sky on a windy day. You could see the taillights glowing through it. I did not know this at the time, but the gentleman who came to my rescue was trying to get the license plate number. "He must be burning rubber," he said almost to himself. He ordered me to get back in the house and lock the door. He started walking towards the car.

"Please do not go up there!" I begged.

The man replied he was not afraid. I asked him what if the other man had a gun? The gentleman stopped and replied he had not thought of that possibility. He shouted to the man in the car, "The police are on their way!" You could hear the other man slam the car door shut and see his taillights disappear as he sped off. He was gone.

The phone was in his kitchen and had a long cord attached to it. Stretching the cord, he handed the phone to me. I dialed my home phone number and handed him the phone back. When my mom answered, he told her I was there, and she needed to pick me up. When she arrived, he told her what had happened and how he was not able to get the license plate. He suggested we call the police and let them know. My mom thanked him, and we left. I was afraid if we went straight home, the man would somehow be in my path again or find out where I lived. My mom questioned me thoroughly, as we headed home. I was so shaken and upset from the whole ordeal I did not think to mention to my mom about the warning I heard.

GUARDIAN ANGEL

As a grown up, I realized the voice I heard above me, warning me at that time, must have been my guardian angel. I believed the knowing of exactly what to do was guidance from my ancestor in spirit. I am certain it was my mom's father, my Pop-pop who was with me. Other mediums have suggested perhaps the warnings may have been the spirit of one of the other girls who did not get away. The directions could have been given by my protector guides. The open screen door and the man inside at home were definitely the Angels doing. These are things to think about as I reflect back on that day.

The first and second warnings were the unseen voice of a male, coming from the heavens. The last warning, heard behind me saying, "He is behind you, run!" sounded like a female's voice. I believe that is why I turned, because I heard it behind me.

I did not go out of the house for a long time after that experience. When I did venture out, I never went out or walked home by myself. I am grateful I had good friends who walked me home.

Shortly after all this, unknown to me, my parents began to receive phone calls from a male who was threatening to do all kinds of unspeakable things to me. My father, of course, offered to meet the caller somewhere and guarantee no one would ever find his body! The things the man spoke of unnerved my father so much he called one of his good friends, who was a detective in the sex crimes unit. The police put a tracer on the phone to try and catch him. Over time, the calls stopped. We had an unlisted phone number, but this person still knew of me. The police were never able to catch the man. At the time, I had no idea this happened. My parents did not tell me as they were trying to protect me from unnecessary worry. During this ordeal, by the advice of the police, no one else was told either. I did not find this out until I was an adult. Who knows? Did I sense the danger because of my being a psychic medium? I feel it does not take a genius to figure out where this fear of being alone stemmed from. Right?

As an adult, looking back, I realized this was when I became afraid of being alone. I did not talk about it, but I found myself going to great lengths to not be alone.

Mediumship Unfolding Naturally

For a natural medium seeing, hearing, and knowing things is as instinctive to us as breathing. When I think about my life now, it all seems so magical in many ways. Yet, in hindsight, the things I could never make sense out of before, now make so much sense to me. It has been an interesting journey to say the least.

My life has been one filled with many interactions with Spirit, Angels and Guides. In between what would be considered a fairly normal childhood, I had experiences with the 'other' dimension. These interactions were a "normal" thing for me. I have come to fully understand and embrace my authentic self. I realized those in the unseen world have been some of my greatest teachers. I say this because, one, it is the truth, and two, because I never had to be told there was an afterlife. I knew it. I was born with that knowledge. What I did have to learn though, was that not everyone has an awareness of this coexistence between us and the Spirit world.

My personal belief is God is the creator of all there is. He has been the orchestrator of all the lessons throughout my life. I have learned it is easier to just go with the flow, surrender, and fully trust I will be taken care of.

Surrendering was a critical piece of my development. I do not mean surrendering, in the sense of giving up, where one waves a white flag. What I mean is learning to trust Spirit. I open myself up, allowing the information to flow through me remaining aware. As the saying goes with mediumship, "From Spirit, through spirit, to spirit."

I am present, in the sense if anything should ever make me uncomfortable, all I would have to do is say, "I am finished now." I do not have to accept the information given as truth. Add to that, "Nor do I have to accept the information as coming from Spirit." For instance, it may have come from my own thoughts. Discerning these thoughts and information is important to be accurately attuned to the highest truth. I do feel the need to mention I fully trust myself, along with knowing I am taken care of when in communication with the other side, always.

I believe the Angels have kept me and my loved ones safe from harm. I believe my Spirit Teacher and Guides have helped me learn how to become a better communicator for spirit. How? As I have mentioned earlier, Spirit will always provide us the lessons we need. If we do not learn, then what? Well, let me put it this way, they do not give up, until we have come to know what we need to learn.

When I refer to Spirit, I mean our loved ones and friends, including our pets, who have transitioned from this earth to heaven. We naturally interact with the spirit world from the very beginning of our lives. Some of us remember these interactions from our earliest memories. You may be wondering how. My belief is when the medium's mind seeks an answer, it is given to us by Spirit. So, for me, being a medium has had its advantages when revisiting those earliest memories. It was one of the keys I used in unlocking those memories from so long ago, combined with what I know, what I am shown, what I hear, and what I feel.

We often are aware of an unseen voice. I believe this voice is our teacher and guide. Sometimes it is referred to as a guardian. The unseen voice can also be an ancestor. My grandmother used to describe this as the little voice inside of you. "Always listen to that little voice inside of you, because it will never lead you wrong!"

Have you ever heard anyone referred to as an old soul? When I was young, my grandmother often referred to me as an old soul. When I questioned her as to what it meant, she explains this meant I was wise, like a little old lady, who lived a long time. Quite often, before I learned not to, I would speak up and say something so profound, it would stop people in their tracks. Many would be left scratching their heads as to how I knew this or that, except me of course! Sometimes I spoke of a solution they needed. I wish I could remember some of these wise things I said! When people like us do this, it is always far beyond our years or our life experiences here thus far.

SIGNS SENT FROM ABOVE

Spirit sends us signs all the time from the heavens, often at that very moment when you think about loved ones, they are closest to us. We do not always trust it even when we smell their favorite perfume or cologne, hear a favorite song or something else that is identifiable. Is it a coincidence or our imagination, we might say to ourselves. Have you ever felt like someone touched your cheek and kissed your forehead?

Look for the signs. They are always there. Take them as the gifts they are. Our loved ones arrange for these encounters, so consider it may not be a coincidence. Consider the energy it takes them to arrange these things.

Sometimes people will receive signs from their loved ones in heaven. After my father died, I started to take notice of this bright red cardinal that would show up. Setting aside all of the jokes of me having ADD issues, it was as if my attention was drawn to it for some reason.

After a while I noticed a pattern. I began to take notice this bird would show up when my mind was filled with so much worry. I pray every day. On this day I had reached out to Mother Mary as I often did in those days and asked her to intervene on my son's behalf. He was so sick with a dangerous virus known as RSV. I had to take him to the emergency room. We were not sure he was going to make it.

My friend came with me to the hospital as an extra set of hands and for emotional support. She knew how worried I was, she was too. Coming out of our housing development, I started to speed up the hill alongside where we lived. Hurrying, when all the sudden out of my peripheral vision I saw a cardinal flying so fast that I had to slam on the brakes or I would have hit it. My friend and I just exchanged a look before she said, "Well, now you know he is going to be okay." True story, and gratefully he was.

Our loved ones send us signs, then our loved ones on the other side nudge us to take notice. Using the cardinal is an example. Our loved ones can arrange to put us in a place where a stranger who happens to be wearing cardinal earrings, will walk up and say something witty to us.

It is important to note our loved ones are not literally the cardinal. Rather, this bird is working with our loved one. Sometimes they can use people to say a particular thing. When you are making an egg and notice a smiley face, it may just be a sign. Or the next time when you are thinking of your loved one and you look up to see a rainbow, or butterflies. It can be when the lights flicker, or you turn on the radio and their song is playing.

The next time your loved one sends you a sign, I ask you to consider it may not just be a coincidence. Especially when we are thinking of them or if we were just speaking about them. By opening your mind to the possibility, you will come to know without any doubt what signs your loved one sends you.

Just a few examples of how our loved ones will send us signs are listed below.

SONGS
- Reminding you of them, your relationship
- their favorite song
- someone else talking about or mentioning the song

BUTTERFLIES
- actual
- pictures
- tattoos
- jewelry

RAINBOWS
- actual
- on suncatchers
- tee shirts
- or in the song 'Somewhere Over the Rainbow'

SMILEY FACES
- actual
- or appearing in the clouds, in food, in puddles of water,
- seeing in pictures

BIRDS
- actual birds of any kind and color
- or in jewelry
- on sweatshirts
- figurines
- or paintings

PREMONITIONS

Premonitions come to prepare us, both positive and negative, for what is written long ago and will certainly come to pass. They are forewarnings of something that is about to

happen. They show up in our dreams to try to prepare us for the inevitable. They can come to us unexpectedly, seemly out of nowhere. For me, those forewarnings, were
always an accurate account of someone's death.

Forewarnings are different from the feeling or sense one may have of apprehension when we are awake. They are different from warnings. As an adult, my premonitions of an impending death come to me through dreams and have always come to pass with no exceptions! The unseen voice, which is the direct voice of spirit, sometimes called an independent voice of spirit, is always with me. This is my guardian, an ancestor, who is my teacher and guide. These insights happened to me so much that I have friends who have jokingly said to me, "Deb, do me a favor will you? Please do not dream of me!" Hahaha, funny I know. Even still, I will tell you all now, I wish it worked like that. I really do!

Every Medium is unique and will have their own experiences and their own lessons throughout their journey for them to be of service to those the Creator needs them to serve. These are my personal accounts of examples of how Spirit communicates with me.

I have chosen to leave my 'own voice' in the stories so you get a 'feel' of me, my emotions and how messages flow through me.

THE DREAM

I woke in a state of panic by my own agonized scream, "No!" I had another premonition in a dream. My mind was desperately searching for any reason as to why I would dream of something so unsettling and disturbing. "Dear God, in heaven," I pleaded out loud, as the realization began to hit me, this dream was about my father! It was as if I were a bystander, helpless, horrified, watching, hearing, and seeing everything exactly how it would happen. In a state of disbelief, I once more cried out loudly, "No, please no! Not my Dad! God, please I beg you! Do not do this to us, or to him!"

I sobbed uncontrollably, because I knew, I just knew. I could deny this, and nothing would change this fact. I was shown, and clearly heard, the unseen voice of my ancestor in spirit as I was told that my father would die. When I asked how, the unseen voice replied. "He will have a stroke." This was torturous! I thought to myself, "This

cannot be, he is only forty-seven for God's sake!"
With all my heart and soul, I did not want this to
be true.

I sat up and before my feet touched the floor,
my rational mind had come charging through
like the Lone Ranger... Hi Ho Silver, away! My
logical mind reasoned, "You're right, this does
not make any sense! The idea is ridiculous to
even think about, he is so young." I was
desperately searching for any reason for this
premonition not to be true. As my mind
continued to spiral into denial, I found myself
thinking I must have misunderstood this. I was
afraid to even speak of it.

Your loved ones in the spirit world
are just a thought away.
- James Van Praagh

Grief

MY FATHER

My Dad was a strong, good-looking man, with
an infectious laugh. He had a brilliant mind and
was devoted to and loved his family more than
life itself. We were lucky enough to know it. Dad
attended Pennsylvania Military College, now
known as Widener University. He majored in
medicine to please his father, who wanted him
to become a doctor. In the end, he left after a
few years. He never wanted to be a doctor.
Instead, he married the love of his life, my
mother, and became a successful businessman
who ran and owned a fourteen-taxicab garage.

At this point in his life, he was transitioning many of the responsibilities over to my brothers and my husband, with plans to retire before he turned fifty.

He was true to himself, never pretentious, spoke his mind and had a generous heart. We were blessed to have a good, healthy relationship with him. He spoiled all of us, and not one of us turned out to be ungrateful. Nothing was impossible. No dream was ever out of his reach. He taught us all by example, instilling his work ethic, devotion, and importance of family in all of us. Life was good in those days. I pushed the dream far away in my mind and locked it up tight. The truth was, it was always there.

MY FATHER'S DEATH

My father died exactly as I had experienced in the dream. Just like my premonition, I was helpless to stop what was happening. I was a witness to it all. Only this time, unfortunately, it was not in a dream. My father died right before my eyes. The memory of this is etched into my mind and emotions. I will never forget. It was a long time before my first thought of my father did not bring me right back to that place, where the horror of it all played over and over in my mind.

As you can imagine, I was devastated. I was confused and furious as to why I needed to know my father was going to die and not be able to prevent or change the outcome. Just like when I was a youngster! Why? I asked hundreds of times over and over. My mind was too tortured and filled with anguish in order to hear any answers.

I threw my gift back to the heavens, declaring in my grief, "You have betrayed me, lied to me and it is cruel. I hate it!" I screamed to the unseen voice and to God. "This gift is not a gift at all! The others were right, it is a curse! God, please take it from me. Take it away!"

THE AFTERMATH

"Why, God?" I wanted to know why. Knowing my father was going to die in advance did not change anything. Yet, his dying changed everything. Just thinking about it now makes my heart ache. The emotional trauma of seeing my father die, coupled with knowing about it beforehand, and not being able to stop it from happening had traumatized me beyond words. All of it was almost too much for me to handle. The last thing I wanted were these abilities. It was exhausting and puzzling.

In my grief, I became overly obsessive compulsive. I strived to do everything perfectly, trying to feel better about what had happened. In my mind, I felt I had failed to prevent my dad's death. I determined if it were in my power, no one would die on my watch again. I wanted to love myself again and I hoped everyone else would love me too. I was hardest on myself. I blamed myself and could not forgive myself for letting this happen to my father. I blamed the medical staff for the unforeseen medical complications I felt contributed to his premature death.

Many memories were locked up in my mind. I was still trying to figure out the pieces to the puzzle. It was as if something would not let me rest. Maybe it was the guilt of not being able to stop my father's death which plagued me? I carried these feelings with me as my penance every day since he passed. I wore the anger I felt over losing him as if it were a badge. I spent so much time deflecting and denying my gifts out of self-loathing because I felt like I failed him. My dad never failed me, not once.

Like a poison, the guilt, grief, and anger burned inside of me. Looking back, I now realize it was almost as if I was trying to kill the part of myself that was the medium. No matter how much I willed those abilities away, it did not stop me from having them. I became good at ignoring them. Just when I thought I had taken care of conquering those gifts of mine, they manifested themselves in another way. I thank God they did.

GRIEVING MY FATHER

Now I know my dad's death was not my fault. I did tell my dad about the premonition dream and tried to talk him out of having the medical test which had indirectly resulted in his premature death. I know, without a doubt, he would not blame me. On more than one occasion, since his death, he has come to tell me, and through other mediums, the choice to have the test was his, not mine. As I sat in the energy of the presence of his love, he reassured me it would not have changed the outcome. No matter how much I would have liked it to change. There were times throughout my grieving process when I imagined different scenarios where I made a scene, ranting and raving, to try make him change his mind. I could almost hear him laughing at the absurdity of these thoughts.

What has brought me comfort is that he knows how much he was loved while he was here and how he was loved by many of us. We love him still.

It was only after my son was born, six months later, I was able to open my mediumship abilities up the tiniest bit. Baby steps. I was grateful my gifts were unfolding in a more positive way during those days and in the only way I would have been able to handle them during that difficult time. I barely had the time to focus on my abilities or anything else because my beautiful eight-pound, six-ounce baby boy was born with a syndrome so rare, only one in forty-four million people worldwide have it. I hope you can see God's sense of humor peeking through here! Are you ready? His syndrome is called Ondines Curse. Did you catch that? A curse! To make a long story short, this syndrome is now called Congenital Central Hypoventilation Syndrome. This means my son has a condition that requires life support while sleeping in order to live a normal life. In order to keep his brain as healthy as possible, seventeen breaths per minute is delivered to him by a ventilator whenever he goes to sleep.

If you are wondering, no, he did not outgrow this. It turns out this syndrome is genetic. Perhaps my ancestors on the other side were working overtime trying to help me heal and get me back on track. Who knows? I felt inspired to explore these weird gifts of mine. Yes, believe it or not, the same ones I had declared were a curse from God, while grieving the loss of my dad.

In those days, my mind was like a human rolodex file, flipping through cards of my memories. Searching, I found myself revisiting the memory of another dream I had one week after my near-death experience. I had essentially forgotten about this dream until my grandmother had reminded me of it while we were chatting one day after he passed. My father was still alive when I had this dream.

During this dream, I was awakened by the sound of loud knocking, followed by a familiar voice calling my name, asking, "Debbie can you hear me?" The familiar male voice would repeat these words over and over again, "Twenty-six,

Debbie this is important. It is your father! Don't forget!" The voice even questioned me, "Debbie do you hear me? It is your father! Do not forget." I did not understand the message and there was no one at my door when I opened it!

At the time, my thinking or conscious mind tried to make sense out of what was happening. Because the voice sounded familiar, I rationalized the voice must have belonged to my Dad.

Why did I not get the message right the first time, with the first dream? The Sherlock Holmes in me had some ideas about all this. At the time of this dream, my body was recovering from a miscarriage, followed a week later with the trauma of a near death experience due to complications of an ectopic pregnancy. This would be the only thing that made any sense as to why I did not fully comprehend the message at the time. I did not think much beyond the connections of my being twenty-six at the time of his death. It would be many years later I would come to understand it was my paternal grandfather who woke me with the loud knocking from the other side.

GRIEF - THE MEDIUM'S ROLE

As a medium, my role in the client's grieving process is one that I do not take lightly. I understand how important it is to stay within the realms of integrity. When delivering a message to a spirit's loved ones, it is important to stay in the energy of compassion. I am not a doctor, nor am I a licensed grief counselor. This is where seeking additional training has been invaluable in helping clients. One of the last things one would want to do is to cause additional grief to the person who is there for the session (known as the sitter). I hold myself to the highest standards, always working in integrity. If I am not able to attain a direct message from spirit, I will not lie and make something up. Throughout my teachings to those I mentor, I have reiterated this as an example. I expect my students to hold themselves to this same high standard. With that being said, the feedback from my clientele has been favorable.

Before reading, I pray the messages will always be helpful and healing for all. Spirit has taught me grief is such a personal thing for each person. How one grieves, another will grieve differently.

Oh, the mistakes well-meaning people have made when trying to find words to comfort people who are grieving. Including myself.

Being of service to those in the afterlife is priceless. It has been my honor to have played an instrumental role, even if only in a small way, to spirit. I can only hope to have been able to provide comfort to those who have sought me out for a reading. This comfort has been validated by many I have read for, knowing their loved ones have survived death by reminding them of the happier times and with the hope of helping them ease their way through their grieving process. This fills my heart with gratitude I was born into this life to help facilitate this healing.

THE STAGES OF GRIEF

Training to become a hospice volunteer, I learned no one has the right to tell someone how they should grieve. Not even me, or spirit on the other side. Spirit can let you know their wishes, however, ultimately you must go through the stages and process.

Grief, and how we grieve, is a personal thing. Everyone goes through the grieving process in their own way and in their own time. As a medium, I often remind those who are going through the process, to not let anyone tell them how they should grieve, including me. Often, I suggest they seek out and utilize various sources of support, such as grief counseling, if they are not already doing so. I refer them to their church or to organizations where they can share their story within the variety of support groups available.

What are the stages of grief? The following illustrates the process that people go through when they grieve.

- Denial, Disbelief, Shock, Isolation
- Anger, Guilt, Pain
- Bargaining
- Depression
- Acceptance

"You were put on this earth
to achieve your greatest self,
to live out your purpose,
and to do it courageously."
- Dr Steve Maraboli

Part Two

Heiress to Unseen Riches

"I could not have made it this far
had there not been angels
along the way."
– Della Reese

Encounters

During my first year of life, I had a couple of close calls. At eight months old, I was bitten by a spider and almost died. Two months later, at ten months or so, I had a bad fall. My paternal grandmother was minding me one day. I learned to walk early at eight months of age, walking all over the place. Nanna had just finished shopping and was putting the canned goods away when my dad dropped me off at her house on his way to work. The neighbor knocked on the door. Distracted, Nan had forgotten to shut the door to the pantry, located at the top of the basement stairs, as she went to answer the front door. Upon returning to the kitchen, my grandmother reacted in fear when she saw me standing at the top of the steps, peering down into the cellar. Unfortunately, her loud gasp startled me and before she could reach me, I lost my balance, falling from the top of the stairs to the concrete floor below. I laid at the bottom of the basement steps on the cold cement and the last thing I heard was grandmother's horrified scream before everything went black.

When my mediumistic mind flows backwards in time to this experience, it is as if I am a spectator watching a scene unfold before me. It is almost like Scrooge's experience in a scene from A *Christmas Carol*. I actually feel like I am there, in that time, observing. As the scene unfolds before me, I see myself lying at the bottom of the stairs, yet I am not in my body when I see this. I was in the middle of the basement looking towards where my name was being called. I could see my grandmother's legs through the railing, hurrying down the stairs. I hear my Nanna screaming my name, trying to wake me, and then the scene goes dark in my mind. I believe this may have been an out of body experience. What do you think?

THE OLD MAN AND HEAVEN

One of the people who used to talk to me was an older man. He used to tell me all about heaven, how beautiful it was and how much God loved me. I do not remember if he ever told me his name or if I ever even asked him his name. He felt familiar to me, especially his voice. It was like I knew him from somewhere and interestingly, he knew my name.

I would come to recognize him as the unseen voice I have heard since infancy. He helped me when I was bit by a spider, nearly dying from a dangerous allergic reaction, and now he was here again. The last time I remembered seeing him was when I misbehaved and was sent upstairs to bed at my maternal grandparents' house, as a punishment for misbehaving.

That day my grandfather was home, and I was being naughty on purpose. Eventually after being warned a few times, he sent me upstairs to bed for sassing back to my Nan one time too many.

It was not long before I felt bad for the way I behaved. For some reason, I found myself thinking about what a few of my friends had told me about 'hell'. They told me that God sent bad people there. I found myself worrying I was not going to go to heaven. It is one thing to do something wrong and not know it, and totally another thing when you knowingly did something wrong.

Lying in bed, I soon drifted off to sleep. I remembered waking up to someone talking to me. "Well, hello there, Debbie!" Rubbing the sleep from my eyes, I saw a man seated next to me at the head of the bed. I sat up next to him as he continued to talk to me and noticed he was not my grandfather.

He assured me no matter what, I was a child of God and not to worry because I would always go to heaven. He added, out of respect for my parents and grandparents, I should not misbehave on purpose, especially to such a good woman like my grandmother. He was right. I felt ashamed of myself. It was almost like he knew how I was feeling. He went on to say there are many rules I would have to learn to follow in order to get along in life, I would make mistakes and it was alright. He encouraged me to forgive myself and to learn from this.

I was feeling much better about everything

because some people told me I would go to hell. I felt they were wrong because God loves us unconditionally. God is not mean! He assured me there was nothing I could ever do to make God not love me. "Really? Nothing? I would still go to heaven?" I was amazed. Isn't that a phenomenal thought? There was never a question in my mind when I was younger. However, other people's religious belief would confuse me as I was growing up. It did not feel like a loving and kind God that I knew.

I wanted to know what Heaven was like. He told me Heaven was wonderful and anything I ever wanted to do, or have, I could have or could just do it. "How?" I asked. He told me all I would have to do is just think it and it would happen, just like that. I was wide eyed, and my brain was thinking how much I liked this news and how much I liked horses. So, I asked him "You mean if I wanted to drive a horse and buggy I could?" He assured me I could indeed.

For some reason I was feeling a little daring and wanted to test the waters. I asked him, "What if I wanted to ride the horse and buggy naked?"

He laughed, "Yes, if you wanted to ride a horse

and buggy naked, in heaven you could, and God would not be mad at you." I believed him. You can see I like to play with my gifts and have a sense of humor.

This made me incredibly happy. I was contemplating how I was never going to listen again, especially if I really wanted something, like candy. While I was thinking this, he appeared to be staring off in front of him. He then said, "Oh dear, I am going to need help with this one. She is not understanding what I was saying." He continued, "Yes, I suppose she is young, but I am concerned about this one."

I was trying to see who he was talking to but did not see anyone. "Who are you talking to?" I asked, wanting to know who he was speaking to.

He looked at me again and replied, "Debbie, this does not give you permission to disobey your elders or the rules in life you are going to have to follow. You are smart, yes, but your elders have lived longer and have had more experiences in life. You have to learn to listen to them when they tell you something. You also cannot be and do bad things on purpose."

"Oh, but you said that even if I were bad

sometimes, God would never keep me from heaven."

Staring off into the distance again he spoke again to someone I still could not see, "See what I mean?" Looking back to me he assured me, "It is okay. It is not your fault. You do not understand." He also told me he was going to have to find another way to teach me.

"Are you mad at me?" I asked.

He looked at me and gently replied, "No I am not mad at you. Go back to sleep now. Do not worry. I will figure it out. Remember to be happy." He touched the top of my head. Lying back down, I drifted back to sleep and when I woke up, he was gone. I felt a wave of sadness.

My grandmother called up to the bedroom, asking if I was hungry. I hurried downstairs thinking maybe the visitor was still there. I looked around, then asked my grandparents where the man was? They asked who I was talking about. I responded, "The man who came and sat on the bed, he was really nice and told me all about heaven." My grandparents just stood there for a moment before telling me I must have been dreaming because no one was at the house visiting. It was just them. I told them the man said he knew them. There was no doubt in my mind the man was actually there. I asked again to make sure no one was there or had come in because it did not feel like a dream to me.

Pop-pop was a quiet man, assured me no one else was home but he and Nana, watching television. They asked me if the man gave me his name. I thought as hard as I could but could not remember his name. I thought it was odd as I did not think he gave me his name. I pictured him in my mind, he had dark hair, thinning on the top, and he wore a black suit. In my mind I saw he had a pocket watch, but I was not sure. "I wish she could remember his name," Nana said to Pop-pop.

"Me too," I replied, "but he told me to not to worry about going to heaven because I will. Everybody does."

I was told to go upstairs and wash up because it was almost time to eat. While upstairs, I could hear my grandmother ask my grandfather, "Who do you think it was?" My grandfather replied that he was not sure but maybe it was his father. When I walked back downstairs, the conversation stopped. Things like 'who do you think it was' were never discussed openly in front of me at that age anyway.

I do not remember ever seeing this older man after that experience, no matter how many times I tried to conjure him. Since I had a vivid imagination, I tried to use it to talk to him, but it did not work. I eventually stopped trying. I miss my friend.

PLAYGROUND WIDOW

One day, I came home from the playground to my mom in the kitchen. She was about to pick up the phone when I sprung this one on her.

"Mom what is adultery?"

"What? Where did you hear that word?" she asked.

"I met an old woman today at the playground, and she told me that word."

"What did she say?"

"That she had committed adultery."

My mother reacted with shock over an adult

telling a child something like that. Not wanting to answer me she distracted me. "Sweetheart, I need to make this phone call right now, go wash up before dinner."

"Okay."

I never did get an answer to my question. However, in my young mind I concluded 'adultery' was not a good thing and probably even a bad word.

This is what I remember of what happened that day. I was sitting on a bench at the playground when I noticed an elderly lady dressed in black from head to toe. She was cutting through the play area, which struck me as odd.

It appeared she was looking straight at me, so I waved to her. There was no response. Thinking perhaps she did not see me I asked, "Hello, how are you?"

She stopped, raised her eyebrows, and replied, "Oh, I didn't think you saw me!" It never occurred to me to ask her why she thought I did not see her. She asked my name and sat down beside me on the bench.

We made small talk and she seemed extremely

interested in my thoughts about God and Heaven. I passionately shared my beliefs with her.

I held a deep belief you had a life review with God after you died. God helps you understand how you made others feel during your life. I did not believe you get sent to hell. I had a knowing you would make restitution.

The woman shared with me she was afraid God would send her to hell. I again reiterated God would never turn his back on her no matter what. She told me she had sinned, that she committed adultery on her husband. I did not know what adultery meant and something told me not to ask her. I just listened. Her concern, she mentioned, was she did not get to confess her sins to the priest and now it was too late.

She also asked me to help. "Tell my daughter I need a candle lit and prayers." She put her hand on top of mine and sat with me a while. When she finally spoke again, she liked my idea of God and Heaven better than hers and hoped I was right. "You are very special, thank you." As she was getting up to leave, she stopped, looked at me and told me she felt much better after talking with me. She patted my knee, said thank you once again got up and left.

Later that evening, my family and I were sitting outside. The neighbors were also outside. I was chasing and catching lighting bugs on our front lawn when I remembered the old lady. She told me her daughter lived on my street and had the same name as her. I was supposed to tell her daughter to light a candle and say prayers for her mom to help her to get into heaven.

Once again, I would have an unusual experience. As I walked up to my neighbor, I mentioned I met a woman with the same name as her. I assumed this was the daughter. I told her about the prayers and lighting the candle. "Oh! Why would she need prayers?"

"I don't know," I told her, "but she said it would help her get into heaven."

She appeared skeptical so she began to ask me a few questions. "What did she look like?"

I described her perfectly, adding, "she even had the same accent as you. She was wearing all black and told me she was a widow." The neighbor acknowledged she sounded just like her mother, but it could not be. Her mother had been dead for almost a month prior to my meeting her. This experience was so real to me I did not know this was an encounter with spirit until much later in life. The widow's daughter discounted me and told me to just go play. I felt like I had let this widow down in some way. Her son-in-law who was standing nearby had heard the conversation. He acknowledged that the woman I had met and described did sound like his wife's mother. Yet she still refused to consider it. I was not validated and let down because I was trying to do a good deed. I apologized for my mistake and turned to leave. However, her husband thanked me. He was quick to tell me that I should never apologize for trying to do a good deed.

A CHILD HAS NO FILTER

There is always a first time when we have that "knowing" come to us. When I was small, I gave someone a hug and kiss goodbye. Out of the blue, without warning, I knew they were going to die. I do not understand how I knew, but I did. I did not remember why I did not say anything to anyone about it. Not long after, they died. When we received the news, I remember thinking, "I should have told them!" I questioned if I had said something, they could have gone to the doctors and would not have died. I felt terrible and responsible. Because of that experience, the very next time I had the knowing, I was determined not to make the same mistake. This time I was going to save them. When Mother's family members were visiting from upstate, to her horror I blurted out, "You are going to die!" What could she say, right?

Embarrassed, my mother quickly apologized. "Debbie do not say things like that!"

"But he is going to die!" My mom, mortified, sent me to my room, again apologizing for my outburst.

After our family left, Mom called me down from my room for lunch. Sitting next to me, my mom nonchalantly asked me, "Why did you say that?"

I told her the first time I knew someone was going to die, I did not say anything and should have. If I did, the doctor might have been able to save them. My mom always thought before she spoke, especially about serious things, unlike me at that age. She explained to me the first person had been sick, and the doctors were not able to do anything more for them. They already were aware they were going to die. "It is not your fault they died. You just knew they were going to die. That's all."

I wanted to know what to do. I asked my mother, "Do I tell them then, if I know?"

"No," she replied. "The reason why you should not tell them is saying something like that can be upsetting for people to hear. If you feel that again, I will tell you what. You can tell me, but not until after they leave. Okay?"

"Okay." I felt much better, and my sandwich was yummy!

After I found out the second person died, I decided I was not going to give anyone a kiss or hug goodbye anymore. I thought to myself maybe I would stay in my room. In my innocent mind, I believed this would prevent me from knowing. Well, I still had a lot to learn. Staying in my room did not work! It did not matter because I still knew.

As I grew older, I continued having experiences like this. After years of shouldering the burden of the knowing and not being able to change the outcome, I asked God to intervene. I was seventeen when I asked him to take this knowing away. I had learned I could not help everyone, even if my heart wanted to. I did not want to know when someone was going to die anymore. Especially, understanding nothing would change the outcome. In gratitude, the way I received information changed. The knowing was still there. However, now I smell the scent of funeral flowers.

I loved going to play with my friend. Skipping over to her home, I was excited to play today. The last time we played together, my friend had been upset and crying because her parents were arguing. We clicked right away because we had our abilities in common, even though she was a little older than me. We were opposite in coloring. I have olive skinned with hazel brown eyes and deep chestnut brown hair. She was blonde, with flawless pale skin and teal blue eyes.

I had asked her why she was so sad. My little friend confided she was worried her parents were going to get a divorce. I knew she was right, and I also knew her father was planning a future with his secretary. She was looking at me waiting for me to confirm. Thinking for a moment I replied, "Yes, you are right they are."

"I knew it," she replied, "and this is all my mommy's fault. I hate her!"

I was taken back by the hate and shocked she was blaming her mom when I knew otherwise. It perplexed me how she did not see the truth, when she was so wise herself. I could feel how much her mother loved her dad and her. I felt nudged forward to discuss the truth with her and spoke up.

When I spoke, I was passionate about defending her mommy. Explaining how this was not her mommy's fault, declaring, "Your daddy does not love your mommy. He is in love with his secretary." This upset my little friend immensely, which made me regret telling her. She thanked me for telling her the truth and assured me she was all right. She asked me to come to her house and play together two days from then.

Two days later I stood on her front steps. When I knocked on the screened door, I could see her mom sitting on the couch. Oh dear, she sounded like she was crying. Before I could turn to leave, she answered the door. I asked if my friend could come out and play. "No, she may not." Oddly, she was speaking with me through the screened door. Normally she would invite me inside to play. I felt confused as she just stood there glaring at me. As her feelings of dislike were oozing from her, I felt it, which began to alarm me. She proceeded to ask, "How did you know and who told you what you shared with my daughter the other day?"

I responded by apologizing. I was thinking how she was being rude by not asking me to come inside to talk. Sensing she was nervous, I noticed she was slurring her words, as she was expressing why she was up all night trying to figure out how I knew. At the age of seven and a half, I had no other explanation other than the truth, "I just knew." The questioning was quite extensive. I was a bit nervous, even though I had innocently shared something I just knew.

"I know how you knew," she announced. Are you ready for this? "You know my husband's secretary, don't you?"

"I can only tell you the truth," I replied, "I do not."

The next words out of her mouth hurt me so badly. "You are no longer allowed to play with my daughter. You are lying!"

"I was not lying," I tried to assure her, endeavoring once more to explain I just knew things sometimes. She told me leave and never to come there again. I was openly crying by this time.

I wanted to know why when she exclaimed, "Because you are evil!" She slammed the main door in my little face.

I could not stop crying as I slowly walked home. My innocent heart felt as though it was deeply injured. I felt it well up as it filled with sadness. Even at the age of seven and a half, I knew she was wrong, I was not evil. No child should ever be told they are evil or feel judged. My inner light dimmed on that day as I walked home toward my safe-haven and family.

Heavy-hearted, I never wanted to hurt anyone. I just wanted to be truthful, as I believed the truth somehow helped people in the whole scheme of things. Even though my friend had asked me to validate what she already knew, I would come to realize my lack of a filter was hurting people.

Now I was judged bad, because of what I said to her daughter. It was the mere fact she thought I was evil because I had a knowing. In those days, not everyone accepted me like my family did. Yes, there were some people who would react positively, smile and thank me. In comparison, many more reacted negatively. Some would freak out, and get mad, others were fearful, and there were those who thought I was evil or cursed.

Fear, ignorance, and self-righteousness reactions towards me, all tried to make me feel less than, beneath them. I have had people react in shock when I shared with them about how much I love God. "You believe in God? Really?" they would ask incredulously. Do not even get me started on the mentality of modern day "witch hunts"! I do not believe having my abilities to sense and communicate with spirit is evil. It is not the dead you all need to worry about. It is the living. Believe me, the dead will never hurt you.

Gratefully, I came to this earth with an innate knowing of God the creator, who I knew as a loving, intelligent and kind being. This is the image of God which was reinforced in my home. Wouldn't it be simple if we could all respect each other's differences without feeling the need to crush one another's spirits, simply because an individual may think and feel "different"?

These were hard lessons for me as a young child. They helped me to learn I must think before speaking about the things I knew. I learned not everyone understood what I knew. I was a good person. I had a clear conscience in knowing I meant no harm. I had always tried to help my friends and family by being honest with them, in sharing what I knew. The time would come when I would gain more knowledge, education, and wisdom from experience and from those who would mentor me.

SPIRIT OF MY PATERNAL GRANDFATHER

Spirit started to visit me again in my mid-teens. These experiences with spirit were different than when I was a small child. When I was about fifteen, the first-time my paternal grandfather visited me an unusual thing happened. I woke up to a strange, almost static electrical sensation. It was a magnetic-like feeling, which literally paralyzed me. Surprisingly, it was not painful. I was unable to move or scream when I saw a spirit-figure of a man standing there in front of me. I grew increasingly frightened, not because of the spirit, but because I could not move.

As my attention was drawn to the figure of the man, I felt there was something familiar about him. He was wearing a blue suit. The suit looked like the one my grandfather was buried in. I no sooner had that thought, when instantaneously there was recognition and a knowing this spirit was my grandfather!

Once I recognized him, and he was assured I knew he was all right, he began to fade and vanished completely, as did the energetic magnetic force holding my body paralyzed. In an instant, I ran into my parents' room like I was six years old, waking up my mother, who then calmed me down and told me to go back to bed.

The next day she wanted to know what frightened me. My mother asked me who I thought this spirit-man was. I replied, "Grandpop Victor". God bless my mom's wisdom as she asked me why I thought it was him. I responded, I thought he wanted to let me know he was all right. My Mother assured me he was all right, replying Grandpop Victor is in heaven.

She asked me why I felt he needed to let me know he was alright. I explained before he died, he was upset because I saw him hemorrhaging the night he woke me up by franticly banging on the wall in our foyer.

Up until that point, my mom did not realize I had seen this. He had throat cancer and had a pulmonary hemorrhage. He had blood leaking into his airway that night. Blood was everywhere as he struggled to breathe. Banging on the wall was his only way of asking for help. When he saw me running to him, he turned and ran away, trying to protect me. I could see this in his eyes, and I could feel this same feeling when I saw him in spirit. My mother listened. She explained there was nothing to be afraid of, and sometimes our loved ones come to us in dreams. It is called a visit. She also affirmed I was right in that Grandpop Victor wanted to let me know he was all right. My mother reminded me there was nothing to be afraid of and to always remember Grandpop loved me and would never hurt me.

RECURRING SENSATION

I have experienced this paralyzing, electrical,

magnetizing energy periodically over the years when spirit has stood at the end of my bed or beside me. This feeling always wakes me up out of a dead sleep (no pun intended.) These 'spells' as we came to call them, would happen before I knew someone had passed, and sometimes afterwards. I even had one on my honeymoon.

I believe these experiences were connected to reawakening the ability of my mediumship as a way of attuning me to spirit energy.

I discovered when I gave up reading for others and when I purposely shut down, ignored, or denied these abilities was precisely the time when the experiences would begin to happen again. Sometimes it would happen several nights consecutively. Spirit was surely getting my attention in this manner.

Many believe we do not choose mediumship. I was born this way, even when I chose to take a sabbatical, and later hearing the call again. I continue to choose to develop my abilities of my own free will. I passionately believe mediumship is part of the creator's plan and part of my life's purpose while I am here.

It Is In the DNA

Very much like someone who has inherited a gift to play a musical instrument, being an athlete or a math whiz, the gift of mediumship runs in families. There are those who become mediums later in life. For now, I am referring to those of us who are born mediums and have others in the family with the same abilities. It is in the DNA.

GIFTS FROM MY MOTHER'S SIDE

My mother was born with a caul, also known as a veil, over her face. This is rare and occurs in approximately one in eighty thousand births.

These children are considered to have the gift of foresight, lucky, and according to folklore, are immune from drowning.

The veil is the embryonic sack encasing the baby inside the womb. When a woman's water breaks during delivery the sack can become fused or stuck on the baby's face mimicking a veil. A full veil is when the baby is delivered inside of an unbroken sack. This is more common in premature births and cesarean births.

Growing up I thought my mom had eyes in the back of her head. She knew everything. My mother was very frightened of her mediumistic gift as a child. This is part of the reason I did not find out about anyone in the family having abilities until after I was married and had two children. I had mentioned to my grandmother, my mother had me taking a card reading class with her and two other friends. You could have knocked my Nan over with a feather! She was shocked. "What? Oh, come on now!" she exclaimed when I told her. She was quiet for a moment and then said, "I am glad she is finally using her gifts."

"What???" Now it was my turn to be surprised, "What gifts Nan?" This is how I found out about the abilities which ran in the family. They were referred to as gifts in my family.

Today using the word 'gifts' to describe the abilities I was born with is looked down upon in our industry. I ask you for your understanding. I do not think I am above anyone, or somehow privileged or chosen by the higher powers. Simply the word gifted, was the word my family used to explain how many of us were.

I was told about my Grandmother's brother (my mother's uncle), who was known to have the gift also. When his father passed away, my great uncle saw him standing in the doorway to their house. He said his father's light was so bright it was like the sun was shining on him. The story goes he had gone outside to gather a few things from the garden for the evening meal. He looked back towards the house and saw his father standing in the doorway, smiling, and waving goodbye. He cried out, dropped the garden tools, and ran towards the house. He knew his father was gone from this earth. He ran past his mother, who was in the kitchen preparing the family meal, to the bedroom where his father was. He kneeled next to the bed, gathered his father in his arms, and mourned him. My great-grandfather had been bedridden and suffering from black lung. He did not have the strength to be able to walk to the door to wave at his son.

GIFTS FROM MY FATHER'S SIDE

I was told my father's aunt was also born with a caul. Unfortunately, I was not told until after she was dead and gone. Nor did I understand at the time she had natural psychic and mediumistic abilities. My great Aunt was a nurse who was married to a police officer. She was not a fortune teller. One day I was talking to my paternal grandmother about seeing my paternal grandfather after he had passed on.

I was on the path of trying to understand more of what was happening to me. My grandmother had mentioned to me and my father that I was like Aunt Annie. As a result of this conversation, she suggested my father take me to talk to her. I did not know this aunt well while growing up. I have few memories of her and now wish I could have gotten to know her better while she was here. At his mother's suggestion my dad had brought me to her home once shortly after I was engaged. Still no one ever used the words psychic or medium. All I was told is my Aunt Annie is a smart woman and I should listen to her.

During this visit, after showing her my engagement ring, she paused while looking at me. Clearly distressed by something she had seen. Seeing her reaction shook me up a bit. I asked her what was wrong? She declared, "I know what you should do, you are going to become a nurse. You will marry a doctor, and your life will be easier!"

I told her I did not want to become a nurse.

She replied "Listen, you do not understand! You will be caregiving anyway, I see it!"

I again informed her I would not become a nurse. In my mind I thought she wanted me to become a nurse because she was a nurse.

She told me, "You think because you can see and you know things, you know everything, but you do not! I have lived longer than you. You still have a lot to learn. I know and I see it. If you marry this man, you will be like a nurse anyway, so you may as well get paid as one!"

I was upset and did not understand why she was saying these things. Respectfully, I stated, "No, I do not want to be a nurse." I had made up my mind.

Years later, I was shutting off my son's alarms to his pulse Ox machine which measured his blood oxygen levels and suctioned the secretions out of his trachea to clear his airway. Seemly out of nowhere, my great-aunt's words ran through my mind. As I watched his oxygen levels rise again to normal range, I looked around his room. There was his crib, a fifty-pound oxygen tank, suction machine, his ventilator for life support and I understood what she meant about what she had seen. If I had a dollar for everyone who had told me throughout the years since my son was born, I should go to school and become a nurse, I would be rich. Right?

NEAR DEATH EXPERIENCE

One December, I had a near death experience, due to hemorrhaging caused by a tubal pregnancy.

I called the doctors' office when I began to have pains. Having experienced a miscarriage four months prior, before becoming pregnant again with my daughter, I was concerned. I had no other logical explanations for the feeling of grief that had welled up inside of me, other than I equated pain during a pregnancy with loss.

With my medical history, the secretary scheduled me with one of the other doctors in the practice straight away. This was before ultrasounds were available or perfected for diagnostic purposes. Since I had not seen this particular doctor before I recapped my previous history including the miscarriage. His response was, "Oh stop worrying! It's normal to have pains in your second pregnancy!" That information did not sound or feel right. I quickly concluded he could not have heard me correctly and repeated myself. Before answering me this time he added how common it was for most first pregnancies to end in miscarriages. He again assured me not to worry.

During the weeks that followed, I had another miscarriage. The doctor performed a D&C and sent me home. I would find myself back in the hospital one week to the day afterward. I was in horrible pain. Unbeknownst to everyone, the pain was caused by an ectopic pregnancy which would lead to nearly losing my life.

One of the last things I remembered at the time was insisting the nurse get my doctor. I was dying and I knew it. My doctor was a sweet man. I liked him the best out of all the doctors in the practice. He arrived at my room and stood beside me. I barely had the strength to speak and he had to move closer to hear me. When he leaned down, I grabbed ahold of his tie. I remember it was yellow and I gently pulled him closer to me. I begged him to please help me, and he replied he had to wait for his partner because he was too old to be doing surgeries. I replied, "You do not understand, I am dying!!!" before I lost consciousness.

I became aware of a man's voice, he sounded upset. I heard someone saying, "Oh my God please help me, I am losing her!!!" I heard him once more, only this time he sounded as if he was farther away as I heard him plead for help. I was in a gray misty area, free. I remember a fleeting feeling of confusion, then I felt as if I were being gently pulled along into the gray mist, which had a bright light. It seemed to be calling me, welcoming me. I was not aware of my body. The gray misty area was almost like you may experience on a foggy day. I traveled towards this welcoming light into another world, a beautiful place. I never wanted to leave this place. I knew this to be true. I was filled with joy. Unlike any joy I have experienced here. I found myself standing next to a being who I recognized as Jesus. Mind you, he did not say, "Hey, I am Jesus!" I knew who He was. I knew I was in heaven. I can tell you without any reservations I have never felt more loved, accepted, and peaceful even though I am very much loved, accepted, and have been peaceful here on Earth.

THE BLISS!

There are no words in our human vocabulary to describe the total acceptance, most perfect pure love, and comforting peace there. The energy of the Creator is present in every aspect. Pure love, which is all knowing, bringing with it a state of bliss. All of this seemed to be radiating within my soul now. The colors were amazing and full of light. Nothing I have seen on Earth could compare, and we have a beautiful earth. They are alive and have a life of their own. They move in vibration to the most beautiful music. The colors seemed to be filling my very essence with the energy of a powerful healing love.

Of course, the being, who I knew as Jesus, was patiently trying to convince me why I should go back to my body and family. We conversed through thoughts, mental telepathy, he showed me everything with living pictures. I was not finished what I had come to earth to do. I was being told things, things that I would forget in an amnesia state if I chose to come back. All I was being told and shown would remain forgotten, until I needed to know, only then I would remember.

At one point, I was aware of my three-year-old daughter standing in front of me, my heart bursting with love for her. I could feel our soul's connection as she was a part of me. When she stood in front of me, her eyes were deep, wise, and soulful. She was trying to convince me to come back. I was struggling with my emotions within because I remembered on a soul level that I was home where I belonged. She calmly asked me not to go, because she needed me. I told her I was going to go, and she will be all right.

"No mom, I do not want you to go. I do not understand why you are leaving me; do you not love me, Mommy?"

I answered from my soul, "Yes, of course I love you." I was aware of her stomping her foot, and pouting.

"Mom, you cannot leave me here with Daddy. You know he cannot take care of me." We both laughed, "Seriously, who is going to take care of me?" I was being pulled, lulled by the peace I craved.

"Grandmom will take care of you and will be a better mom to you than I could ever be." I knew that because she was my mom. I reassured her, "You know I love you. I love you with all my heart, but I belong here, not there. I am happy here. We will see each other again."

"This is not what I want Mommy," my daughter's brave little soul told me, "but I will respect your decision. I wanted to see you before you go and let you know that." I felt her energy pull back from mine, letting me go.

I felt cocooned in the energy of heaven again, resting and healing from all that I had experienced, felt, was shown, and told. I was being shown things again. Like how I had not finished what I came here to do. How I had a son who was to be born yet. These things were all part of my purpose in this lifetime. I was aware of being told if I wanted to stay there I could. The choice was mine to make. I wanted to stay there in heaven.

Jesus appeared again saying, "Look! Look at your mother." I felt myself aware of my mother in front of me. Observing her, I saw she had a look of devastation on her face. Her light was dimmed, she seemed almost broken.

"Why is my mother so broken?" I asked Jesus.

I heard, "Ask her."

"Mom!" my mind called out, I felt her soul energy as I knew her, I felt her love, and her strength. She was compelling me to look at her. When I did, I had total understanding without any words spoken. My mother's gaze held mine, I felt her tremendous pain as she begged, "Please do not do this." Suddenly I felt a strong, "NO, DO NOT GO!"

It was pivotal moment. I was given a choice as

to whether or not to come back.

Concurrently, Jesus had shown and told me things would not be how I thought they would be if I left now. I was given so much knowledge, and a look into their futures. Now I knew why my mother would not be in my daughter's life if I choose to leave and what would have happened to my daughter without me or my mother in her life. I knew instantly why I had to go back. That was when I fought like a champion to come back. Next, I was aware of a man's voice encouraging me saying "YES THAT'S A GIRL FIGHT! KEEP FIGHTING! FIGHT!"

I have a vague memory of being woken up briefly, but I must have still been heavily sedated. As I became aware of my body, I felt like the pain in my chest was killing me. It felt like I needed to breathe deeply and could not get enough air into my lungs. As I tried to take a deep breath in, I felt instantaneous pain. Had someone beat the hell out of me? I did not care because I was being pulled back into a dream state.

While not fully awake, my mind sensed something as I felt warm water and soothing strokes on my body. The strokes felt like heaven.

Somewhere I could hear low murmurs of two voices talking quietly amongst themselves. Feeling the sudsy warm water made me realize I was being washed. Slowly I opened my eyes to see if I was still in heaven. Instead there were two women at my bedside. I asked who they were and the one on my left-hand side said they were nurses who were bathing me and then going to massage me. The one on my right side began to ask me if I remembered anything.

About what? I replied. In my mind, I was thinking, "Oh if I tell you, you are going to give me one of those white jackets that tie in the back!" I heard laughing. To this day I do not know if I said that out loud or not.

They laughed again, just as I thought to answer their question with a question, "Why is my chest hurting so much?"

One of the nurses replied, "You are going to be sore because you have been through a lot and had a hard time in there."

I asked where? The other woman shushed her. I felt lulled someplace else as they were massaging me. I heard again "What do you remember? Do you remember anything?" I must have drifted into a deep sleep because they were not there when I woke up again later.

The next time I woke up, my husband was there with a worried look on his face. Seeing my eyes open eased the worry on his face. He was glad to see me awake and proceeded to tell me how I scared the hell out of him. In fact, he informed me, I scared the hell out of everybody, even the doctor. "Really?"

I listened as he described to me how the doctor came straight out of the operating room to talk to him and all he heard was, "Listen, we had a hard time in there. Your wife lost a lot of blood."

At that point, all he could see was the doctor's lips moving and he could not focus on what the doctor was saying. The doctor's scrubs were covered in blood. My blood. Shocked at the sight before him, his mind searching, he questioned, "Is that my wife's blood? Oh my God."

My husband said he felt like he was going to pass out. He tried looking away to the floor, trying to focus on what was being said, that is when he noticed blood all over the doctor's shoes too. He could barely speak. Quietly, he asked the doctor if I had died.

The doctor replied, "No, she is alive, we were able to stabilize her, but she lost a lot of blood."

"I can see that," my husband commented.

The doctor apologized for not changing beforehand. My husband asked if I was going to be all right. The doctor's answer to him was, "I think so, but I do not know for sure. There were a lot of bleeders, but I think I was able to get them all."

My husband, startled, asked nervously "What do you mean, you THINK you were able to get them all?"

The doctor again tried to reassure him he did the best he could do under the circumstances. He followed up with, "We will have to wait and see. She will need a blood transfusion but for now she is stable."

It seemed my psychic senses were almost supercharged after the near death in some instances. For example, when the doctors came to talk to me about getting the blood transfusion, I flat out refused. The reason being I heard a clear, "No, *the blood is not safe here.*"

A few weeks later I was watching the news. The

reporter was saying one of the top blood donors, a surgeon from the very same hospital, had been diagnosed with AIDS. The blood type was the same as mine. I will never know if the warning was just a knowing or not. In those days as compared to now, there was less known about treatments. Many died.

The practice of Mediumship provides proof of the souls' survival after physical death takes place. We will see one another again in heaven. This is our souls promise to one another. The medium is providing a peek into the afterlife, we have to stand in integrity. Healing and mediumship are a large part of what our belief is based on. I was baptized Lutheran, and consider myself a Christian, as well as a Spiritualist. Before I embraced spiritualism, I practiced the Catholic religion, marrying and raising my children in this faith.

SPIRITUALISM – SHARED TRADITION

I mentioned that Spiritualism has been a source of support and affirmation for me. Most people know little about it because it is not a large group when compared with mainstream religions. The quote below gives some background on the roots of Spiritualism. You will understand why, as a natural medium, Spiritualism has meant so much to me.

Most of the various forms of psychic phenomena associated with the Spiritualist movement are as old as man himself. Throughout the ages human beings have been aware of the existence of discarnate beings. In early days, when man lived close to nature, ancestor-worship became a form of religion; primitive man had no doubt that his ancestors had survived death and that they had powers to affect the living for good or ill.

The early Christian Church was founded on the basis of mediumship, Jesus of Nazareth being considered to have been an exceptionally gifted psychic and medium, as illustrated in the reports of his healing powers, inspired teachings, and so-called 'miracles'. After the Crucifixion it is recorded that Jesus was seen and heard by Paul and others and it is clear that mediumship played an important part in the work of the Apostles in the spreading of this new religion

and its presentation in Church services.
https://snui.org.uk/historyofspiritualism.php

Spiritualism is not all about mediumship.
The Seven Principles of Spiritualist philosophy
reflect this:

1. The Fatherhood of God.

2. The Brotherhood of Man.

3. The Communion of Spirits and the
Ministry of Angels.

4. The Continuous Existence of the human
soul.

5. Personal Responsibility.

6. Compensation and Retribution hereafter
for all the good or evil deeds done on earth.

7. Eternal Progress open to every human
soul.

The philosophy is inclusive and embraces
persons from all walks of life and faiths. You will
notice that the principles are written with old-
fashioned phrasing. That is because modern
Spiritualism came about in the United States
when the Fox sisters, Margarette and Catherine,
of Hydesville, New York, were able to
communicate with a spirit that had been making

rapping sounds in their home. The year was 1848.

Interest in this phenomenon and its implications spread across the country and over the ocean to Europe. Even Mary Todd Lincoln, President Abraham Lincoln's wife, delved into it due to the loss of her beloved son. The history is fascinating and broad. For this book, I wanted to provide some background for you to understand more about my acceptance of a faith group little known to the general public.

CONFUSION

Young and old individuals alike have been leaving the philosophy of many religions behind. This has been happening for many years for a variety of reasons. Why? I do not have all the answers as to why. I just have my own personal experience. Growing up I went to more than a few different churches looking for the God I came into this world knowing. What led me there were the friends I was associating with at the time. We all shared the confusion of a loving God who, at the same time, was feared for being vindictive and judgmental. Some of these churches were Protestant, others Catholic.

I even took Jesus into my heart and was saved. All the church services I attended held a deep love for God. However, the part that never resonated with me was the forceful, vindictive God. Personally, this did nothing but turn me off from those types of teachings and confused me. I felt like I was being lied to. As a young adult this confusion turned into doubts. I became conflicted over whether my abilities were from the devil, or God. It was other human beings who reinforced things which had just happened as being negative, or evil.

Then there is the time when we send our children into the education system. They will learn all about the advancements of science. Both myself and my children were taught by the institution which educated us, we exist because of evolution. I just want to state my truth, even if science is correct, this does not mean there is no higher power.

In both instances with religion, and education, I feel it is worth a reminder to keep the dialogue open with your children. Remember when you learned these things, ask yourself what did this create in your mind? What was the intention behind this part of our religion, or education? For some even with discussion this can create doubts, eroding little by little any hope of an afterlife.

For the record, I am not assigning blame to anyone or anything. This is what happened to me. Those seeds of doubt were planted, and life happened. People gave me their opinions of why my children were born with medical issues and even told me how my father was in hell. I wondered what it was about me which gave them the impression they could say these things to me? Guess what? I am a child of God! The last I checked in His infinite intelligence; the same God that made them has also made me. It is that intelligence I choose to associate myself with, in my daily life and when being of service to those on the other side.

I soon removed myself from those so-called friends. Now, I surround myself instead with people of all faiths, and belief systems who share the common denominators of decency, integrity, and respect for others.

When I say something mediumistic to a non-medium, sometimes the reaction is one of awe, other times the reaction is fear. Instead of considering the possibility of this being possible, some people who have abilities like mine, have been labeled crazy or even schizophrenic. This can cause a knee jerk reaction to what is not understood. This pure ignorance, or at least I hope that is where the type of name calling stems from. This is still happening in our own society today and even in some of our homes. In the world of psychology today, many are aware there is a difference between mediumship and psychiatric issues.

For the record, I have never been diagnosed as crazy or schizophrenic by any professional I had sought therapy from over the years. What I did learn through therapy was I have certainly reacted to being triggered as anyone would have been under those circumstances. Once I understood what those triggers were, why, and in what way they triggered me, I was able to move past them. I have been called these names. As an adult I had to relearn how to stand strong and be confident in who I am, no matter what others thought, said, or did. People are entitled to their opinions. However, I am entitled to the same respect as you would expect from me.

THE GIFTS GO ON - MY CHILDREN

My daughter would often see her grandfather in dreams after he died. I was fascinated when she told me one day how my dad would come to her in a purple light and take her flying. "You had a dream about grandpop, I asked?"

"No Mommy, I was not dreaming. Grandpop visits me all the time," she insisted.

"I believe you, and believe Grandpop does visit you," validating her experience. I always encouraged her to tell me about her visits and I would listen attentively.

"He takes me flying!" They would fly way up into the sky, all around the stars while he told her all about heaven. She told me how much she was learning from him. "The moon isn't really made of cheese, Mom!" She was so serious. When I inquired as to what else she was learning, her answer simply was, "Grandpop is teaching me all about heaven, Mommy!"

From what I could gather from her as a four-year-old, my father had told her that one day soon she would forget these times where they flew and he told her about heaven because she was a child.

As I listened to her, I was touched at how much joy these 'visits' brought her. I was nudged to grab my journal and write this all down. I am so glad I did, because I knew these experiences were real visits and interactions with my dad, her grandpop's spirit. At the time of his death, she was his only grandchild. As an adult she has received signs which left her heart joyful when she needed it most.

WE NEED TO GET HOME

One night where I was working, my daughter had filled in for the regular hostess. I was heading towards the desk when my daughter and I almost collided. She looked upset, so I asked her what was the matter? She said, "We need to get home Mom."

I said, "Yes, I agree."

"I have a bad feeling," she told me. She felt like someone had a heart attack, and had just died, adding, "It's really bad, Mom."

I told her about the thought of who had popped into my head. The thought would not go away. I asked her who she thought it was, and she said she was not sure, "Just that it was really bad." She specifically said, "I feel like someone had a heart attack."

I thought of my grandmothers, they both had bad hearts. We left and carefully drove towards home. We were not on the road long before my husband was calling my cell phone. He said our niece had died; they thought she may have had a heart attack. He was on his way there now. She was only twenty-six and left behind four children. When we arrived home, my son met us at the door. He was visibly shaken. At the time of my niece's death, a glass bottle that was displayed on top of the upper kitchen cabinets in our home had spontaneously shattered when there was no one near the display.

MY SON'S DREAMS

My son also had experiences throughout his life with the knowing. He had a vivid interaction with an Angel in a dream. The Angel said she wanted to show him something. She showed him brand new expensive sneakers, skateboards, tattoos and so forth. The Angel put those things in a very dark and scary place. In this dream, the place was somewhere he may never come back from. Now mind you, he was in second grade at the time of this dream and I am glad I wrote it down.

What do you think I was hoping at that point when he was telling me about this dream? He would make the right choice, right? He went on saying, how he did not care because he really wanted all these things. The Angel warned him again. He said the Angel just watched as he dove headfirst right into this dark, downward pit. He became aware of a horrible demon monster and it was going to kill him. He said he was so scared. He said, "I changed my mind but there was nowhere to run!"

He said the next thing he knew the Angel was there swooping him up. I was fascinated by this vivid dream. He said, "The Angel flew so fast Mom! Even she was scared because she didn't think we were going to make it." He said she used all her might. He thought the demon monsters were going to kill them both. She flew away so fast, even while the demon-monster was only inches away from her feet, until they were gone, and he was safe.

The day he told me about this dream, I had asked him what the Angel looked like. He described her with long brown hair and wearing a long blue gown. "Oh, come on," I said. "I have on a blue nightgown and have brown hair."

"I know Mom, but so did she." Later in life, I would learn a healing modality where you work with the Angels.

While in elementary school my son had another dream, much like a scene in the movie, *Sixth Sense*. He again was visibly upset at what he had seen. In high school, sadly, he lost those same three friends in the same manner as shown to him in the grade school dream years before.

Natural Mediums are known to have vivid dreams. If not written down, some dreams as well as incidents may be forgotten. I would suggest to parents to take the time either to record or write down their children's experiences and dreams. They often have great insights. Later in life, you will be able to remind them of the childhood expression of their knowing.

Both of my children had mediumistic experiences and dreams. I encouraged my children to share these experiences with me, keeping an ongoing clear dialogue with them about what they encountered. I am glad I wrote them down at the time my children were young so the memory wasn't lost.

HAVING ME FOR A MOTHER

I was down at the beach with my husband and son. Our daughter was working and was going to join us in a few days. Out of a dead sleep I woke up, grabbed my phone, and called my daughter. I knew she was scared and needed me. My husband also woke up and started asking me who I was calling at two thirty in the morning. Our daughter, I answered. I ignored whatever else he was saying, as I did not have time to explain myself because she answered.

"Hello?" She answered, "Oh Mommy thank God you called me. There is a man following me and my friend, I'm so scared." I knew not to hang up with her. I told her to stay calm, ride towards the police station, tell them what happened and to continue to talk with me as they headed there.

She said she was giving her friend a ride home and noticed a car had seemed to be following them. Every time she made a turn, the car made the same turn. At one point, she thought she lost them. When she pulled down her friend's street, this car pulled up close behind them. Afraid, she sped out of the development, and the car followed her. "Then you called me," she said.

In my mind, I saw a state police car, sitting in the parking lot of a local store. "Okay, listen. Do not drive to the police station. When you drive by the local store, look and see if there is a State Police car there. If so, pull up next to the police car, scream, make a lot of noise and have the trooper help you."

"Yes, Mom there is a State police car there." The car took off when they pulled into the parking lot.

Interestingly, after sharing this part of my book with my family during its drafting stages, Mom shared with me she also had a similar experience

as a teenager. Reflecting upon this, I feel
sometimes our goodness can attract the
opposite. I feel these experiences reinforce the
importance for us to listen to that inner
guidance and be discerning.

MY HEAD HURTS

Once, I had gone out for the day with a friend
of mine. We went to South Philadelphia while
our kids were in school. We had a great day. On
the way home, I felt like I banged my head and it
hurt. My friend, sensing something was amiss,
asked me what was wrong. I responded by asking
her to please hurry home, because I had a feeling
my son was hurt. She asked me how I knew, and I
told her I felt like I was hit on the head. To be
fair, my friend has always been understanding
and patient with me, until that moment. She told
me I needed to knock off this crap. My son was
fine, and I needed to learn how to relax. She also
told me I was going to make myself sick if I "kept
this up".

I knew her heart was in the right place, out of
care and concern for me. The two of us have
been good friends for years. As we pulled up to

the house, my head was killing me. In one specific spot, I felt a burning sensation. The bus quickly arrived and when my son got off the bus, he was holding his bleeding head. As it turned out, one of the kids on the bus whacked him in the head with a book. There was a scuffle and my son was pushed backward. He banged his head against the metal sides of the opened window. The bus driver stopped the bus and pulled the kid off him and separated the boys. My son did not tell the driver, or anyone else, he was bleeding and hurt. However, I knew it and I felt it.

Part Three

It All Comes Together

We all have a beautiful light within...
We just sometimes forget it is there.

– John Holland

Psychic and More

I BECOME A CARD READER

I had booked a card reader to read for a group I was having over at my house. Kathy, a woman I did not know very well, had given me the reader's number at a ceramic class we attended. It was the first time I had sat with her and her friend. She was finishing the last touches on a pair of ceramic swans she was making for her sister's upcoming wedding. Earlier, I had overheard her and her friend talking about a card reader. She had overheard me talking about my children and complemented me on what a good mother I was. She understood my concerns for their wellbeing.

"I can tell how much you love them," she said. She had a young son whom she loved to the moon and back. Her face lit up when she talked about him.

We chatted about the children, and eventually the conversation led back to the reader, who she highly recommended. I asked for the reader's contact information. She had taken the time to handwrite a note with the reader's name and number. On the bottom of the note, she wrote, "I know this woman is going to help you in some way." I had promised at the time to book the reader. Months went by before I did. I mention this because it is an example of how our lives are intertwined and perfectly planned out by the Creator. It turned out the card reader became my teacher, showing me how to read the cards. I studied under her direction for about four years, going from beginner to advanced levels. Expanding my knowledge base past traditional Tarot card reading into studying astrology, the runes, and past lives with her.

She was instrumental in getting me started in the business. An important lesson I learned from her and have put into practice myself is how important it is to support your students. This teacher took me under her wing because she believed in me. She was very generous with her praise and with helping introduce me into the field.

Remember, Kathy, the woman who gave me the card reader's information? Shortly after our chat, she lost her battle with breast cancer and passed away. She was such a good, sweet soul, no one would ever know she was so ill. I kept feeling nudges to book this card reader and I am glad I did. If it were not for her, I would not have met the woman who became my teacher. If you think that is beautiful, wait until you read the next sentence. Unbeknown to any of us at the time, many years later my daughter would meet and eventually marry Kathy's son! True story. Is your heart smiling? I know mine is. Thank you, Kathy. She was a true Earth Angel.

ARE YOU PSYCHIC?

The first time someone asked me if I was psychic, I seriously had never heard the word before and had to ask them to define it. To describe myself as sheltered and naïve would be accurate. Once I knew what it meant to be a psychic, I answered yes. Adding that I have been psychic my whole life.

One day I was talking to a colleague who had become a good friend. He had been my first mentor who taught me about the Angels. He had a lot of experience and knowledge. I had not known there was a difference in the way one would give Mediumship readings verses Psychic readings. The night before I had given a reading to another card reader who demanded to know exactly what card had told me her father was in spirit. I was caught off guard and struggled to explain myself. I had felt his presence and he had impressed upon me the circumstances of his passing. My friend explained the difference between being a psychic and being a medium. It was through sharing this scenario, when I realized all those seeming coincidences were encounters with spirit. He helped to assure me, that I was a natural medium as well as psychic. When looking back at it all, things became so clear to me and made sense. I knew he was right

Many years would pass, before I would take a

much-needed sabbatical from the metaphysical world altogether. In the meantime, I was slowly cutting back working as a psychic medium. I found myself calling my friend and fellow reader to fill in for me more and more often. This made it easier for me to finish school and transition into another career.

I feel it is important to those of us who work in the field to have other colleagues, or mentors we can discuss our experiences with. This can be essential in helping each other problem solve with both clients and experiences we are having.

MASSAGE SCHOOL, FACILITATOR AND OWNER

I considered going back to school to become a Physical Therapist. After deciding I did not want to go back to school for six to eight years of additional schooling. I was feeling a little lost. I said a prayer asking for direction. Not long after I heard about massage therapy. I have to be honest I still was unsure. I had never even had a massage before. Talk about talking a leap of faith. I thought about it and felt this idea resonates with me. During the interviewing process I found out the director who would be my instructor was a Reiki Master. We clicked immediately. In what seemed like no time at all I found myself enrolled in a massage school.

After graduating, and not being qualified to work in the medical field. I decided to attain experience and continuing education. While doing so I was also able to utilize the cosmetology license. The one I had insisted on holding on to all those years even though I was no longer using it. I worked in the salon industry providing both therapeutic massage, skin care, manicures, and pedicures. I became a National Board-Certified Massage Therapist and Bodyworker, shortly after graduating, and when state licensure was passed, I became state licensed as well. I was on my way to working in the medical industry with massage therapy.

I soon had the vision of opening a massage school. I developed a Therapeutic Massage and Bodywork program, and opened a school for therapeutic massage and bodywork, licensed by the state's Department of Education. It came as a solution to help fill a void which had been growing within me since giving up reading. I had a dream and manifested it. To my husband's credit, he supported me, even though he could not fathom how in the world I was going to start a school. He soon warmed up to the idea after talking to the commercial realtor who found us the perfect properties.

So many blessings came out of those years. One blessing came in the form of being a guest speaker on a local radio show. I shared my expertise on the benefits of myofascial release and other massage modalities with their listeners. The show was led by the doctor I had worked for several years. It was there where I provided medical and rehabilitative massage on their patients in between instructing at the school. The radio experience helped to prepare me for a future radio show WDEL 101.7 FM where I would give mediumship and psychic readings to their listeners.

I had become a certified hospice volunteer, providing services to hospital staff and patients. This experience was enriching, knowing I was instrumental in alleviating any discomfort to those who were dying or transitioning as we call it. Honestly, this also further increased the compassion and empathy I had towards those who were suffering and was made more aware.

How has all this helped me become a better medium? Anytime you increase your knowledge base in any way it helps you be a better communicator for those in heaven. Spirit will use the mediums knowledge and experiences to communicate through us. For example, all the anatomy I taught; spirit uses to show me different ailments people died from.

There were times I felt bad leaving mediumship only to discover later on this had been another opportunity to expand upon my knowledge base. Even when we travel or speak another language, this is beneficial to those who use us for their voice.

While being a wife, mother, daughter, and friend I still managed to earn a good reputation as an Institution, and educator, both within the state and industry. Employers were always calling my school and asking for our graduates. It was through owning and training individuals that I was finding a purpose outside of my family life. I met people who valued me, liked me, and were happy to see me on a daily basis. I enjoyed the experience and confidence boost of students being happy to see me. I would look back upon these times years later and understand each step was preparing and giving me experience to use in the future.

As much as I tried to shut my abilities down, it did not stop me from having psychic and mediumistic experiences. Instead, I was able channel my abilities in different ways, using my gifts to create programs and new ways to keep the students inspired. However, try as I might to not be who I am, it did not work. I was called back to be of service to spirit again. This time, feeling a need for education and credentialing, I was led to the path of evidential mediumship, trance mediumship and trance healing. A part of me did not want to let the school go because of all the good we did for the community. I asked God and the Angels to send the perfect buyer for the school when the timing was right.

A CALL I COULDN'T REFUSE

One night, sitting quietly at home, I was clearly told I would be going back into mediumship in the future. I was told during this meditation that many more mediums were going to be needed because in the future "people would be leaving the planet in droves."

I remembered having a moment of sheer panic. "Oh, come on now God, I cannot just close down everything I fought so hard to build! I have obligations. This is not just about me."

"Trust", I heard, "You are exactly where you are supposed to be." I was told that all of us who would serve were being prepared for when the time arrives.

I did not question this as it rang true to me, even though I did not understand why.

In the years following, what I was told has come to pass. Many have left with the ongoing opiate crisis. Now with the COVID-19 pandemic, and perhaps more yet to be known events.

A part of me did not want to let the school go because of all the good we did for the community. I asked the Angels to send the perfect buyer for the school when the timing was right. They did!

FORMAL TRAINING IN MEDIUMSHIP

I decided if I were going to come out of the spiritual closet, I would need to attain credentialing. In the process of seeking mentors, teachers, and tutors, I attended many workshops, conferences, and training seminars with respected and well-known mediums. Opportunities lined up almost magically!

The first professional Mediumship course I had taken was with a well-known medium, who worked with the Angelic realm. I loved her work. I was fortunate enough to have attended one of her last live angel certification courses before she retired.

I became certified and attuned to the Healing Angel Energy known as Integrated Energy Therapy®. I practiced this healing modality diligently. Eventually, after completing the Master Teacher Levels, I went on to teach the method and continue to do so. In 2012, I was recognized as one of the top thirty teachers internationally. This recognition came from Stevan Thayer, owner of the Center of Being, and the creator of Integrated Energy Therapy®.

Following that, I was blessed to have trained under top-notch, amazingly gifted mediums, healers and teachers. I was led to the path of evidential mediumship, trance mediumship, trance healing and Spiritual healing. I traveled to England, studying at the famous Arthur Findlay College in Stanstead, England. After a year-long intensive program, I became a Certified Spiritual Teacher, rounding out my credentials. As an educator, I knew and understood the value of credentialing being as important as experience.

IN THE MEANTIME

I kept this all to myself while trusting when the timing was right, I would know. In between all this time, much would happen which brought changes into our lives before I would be able to pursue this calling wholeheartedly. My son almost died. Within a year of one another both my mother and husband would almost die. Gratefully this was not their time to transition. My time was freed up, I was able to be their caregiver while they recovered. I feel like our Creator recognizes care giving is part of this journey, for some of us anyway.

When I made the firm decision to come back out of the spiritual closet, the Angels, who I had invited into my life many years before, instantly went about helping to manifest all the right people and situations to support this decision. While waiting for the school to sell, my plans would be kept within the safe cocoon of those closest to me, and of course the Angels. Going back into the metaphysical world of mediumship was in the makings, as was the component of mentoring others. I was looking forward to getting back to that part of my soul-self I had denied so long. The medium, the healer and the teacher, were emerging like the butterfly!

The desire to develop my gifts of mediumship filled me with such happiness and excitement I had not felt in a long time. I was guided to an interactive workshop held in Scottsdale, Arizona, where three very well-known international psychic mediums, and international soul coach would be teaching the participants!

The invitation showed up by postcard in the mail. I took it as a sign as the woman who was running this as a retreat was doing so in honor of her mother, Ariel. I worked closely with Angel Ariel, and the healing Angels. To boot, they were having an Angel Party, and offering an extended schedule for those interested in taking additional workshop training on top of what was already included.

When I arrived the hotel was welcoming and the rooms were perfect! Once the seminar began the atmosphere was charged with so much positive energy and the room was filled with people who belonged to my soul tribe. You know what I mean? Those people who you feel like you have known all your life? I suppose we all knew each other in heaven.

Sharing time with like-minded individuals, who have many of the same beliefs as I did was so nice. I could let my hair down and be my woo-woo self. Seeing so many who worked professionally as mediums, psychics and soul coaches was encouraging. As an educator myself, I found their training to be top notch! I was in my glory, feeling at home there amongst my peers.

While there, I attended the Angel Party. It was divine! During one of the psychic medium demonstrations, I was blessed enough to receive an excellent reading! The medium's evidence was superior, as far as accuracy was concerned.

In addition, the heartfelt message I received moved me. I could feel the presence of my loved ones there with me in those moments shared. My family in Spirit came to tell me they were supporting me from the other side. They were proud of me for doing this work. It felt wonderful to know they were supporting me from the other side. I would advise those who feel they have the 'gift' to embrace it and develop their abilities even if they are not interested in doing this as a profession. It will help them understand themselves better.

A WELL-EARNED PLACED ON THE STAGE

My years working as a professional medium had helped me gain experience and wisdom. The women on the stage earned their place there, and I had the honor of being taught by them. I still had so much to learn and desired more education so I could be of better service to the spirit world. The whole experience was so healing. I was reminded I also wanted to heal people.

For months afterwards I was still filled with all the supportive healing energy this experience gave to me. One of the more profound healings I experienced was the help, through information that explained my experiences. I was encouraged to accept my gifts as part of my purpose. To be proud of who I was born to be and to own it! There were more healings which would continue to unfold for years to come.

There has never been a doubt in my mind Angels exist. However, my understanding of their purpose was limited to your Guardian Angel, and their purpose in the Bible. One of my clients had brought me a book, *Angels* by Charles Capps, as a gift after I had helped her locate her son who was missing. She had bought it at a bookstore called "The Word" across the street from our church, Saint Joseph's.

She wanted me to read this book as she explained God made the Angels to help us, adding we could ask them for help with all sorts of matters. It was a thin paperback I read in two evenings after putting my children to bed. I did not know how I felt about asking the Angels to do things for me. I had always prayed to God for everything I needed. However, I read the book and found it interesting. It explained the hierarchies of the angels and expanded my knowledge on this topic. Afterwards I did not give it much thought as my life was busy with taking care of everyone else and working.

LEARNING ABOUT ANGELS

One evening, a coworker asked me to come along with her to learn about the Angels. To be honest at first, I was hesitant about going. I told her I would need to think about it. Sure enough, when contemplating as to whether I should go or not go an Angel appeared within the eye of my mind. She was beautiful and looked like a Disney hologram. She had long red hair with an emerald green head band to match her long emerald green dress. In her arms she held a sleeping child wrapped in a white blanket. I could not believe it! I was beyond excited about seeing this vision.

As soon as I saw my coworker, I explained I had received my answer and would be joining her and another of our coworkers who was also interested. I would end up becoming good friends with the teacher and I am grateful to him for all he taught me. We had worked together for a couple of years and he is the one who also explained to me I was also a medium and not just a psychic.

It was something I would not soon forget. On

the first day of class, the knowledgeable, gentle teacher asked each of us to pick a card. Guess what? The Angel on my card had red hair and was holding a baby. Let us just say, I was hooked from that day onward!

I have learned so much from working with the Angels. The Angels have said even though we have named them different names, they are all one. I have come to know the same is true of us in the sense we are all connected to one another. We are all one.

I slowly transitioned from a massage school/ business owner and teacher to retirement.

I quietly put it out there I was looking for a buyer for my massage school so I could retire. I was looking forward to retiring and embracing being a full-time grandmother. I began to prepare by cutting back on the school schedule. During all this, I was continuing to prepare to be of service to spirit through mediumship and healing. Always, in my mind was "the Call" I had heard from the Creator and Spirit during that meditation a few years back.

One night, while working late at the school, out of the corner of my eye I became aware of something that appeared. For a brief moment, I thought perhaps I was losing it. I looked anyway and saw the spirit of a tall, thin, older man with bright white hair and blue eyes. He was dressed in a deep shiny midnight blue shirt which reminded me of the stars in the night sky and pants to match. To me this is what made his coloring stick out in my mind. He did not speak to me, not one word. Then, as fast as he appeared, he disappeared. Quick, in a blink of the eye, gone! I felt like I knew him somehow. I remember thinking perhaps he was an Angel.

During this period, I had been facilitating a lot of workshops teaching Integrated Energy Therapy®, (IET®). IET® is often described as Healing with the energy of the Angels. Keep in mind I am also a natural Medium, so I did not think it odd to see an Angel, or any spirit for that matter. Deciding to keep this to myself, as I often did in those days, I did not tell anyone else about it. I jotted it down in a notebook. However, he kept appearing and only when I was at the school. He followed the same pattern: appearing, not saying a word, then disappearing. I became more and more curious.

THERE WERE TIMES WHEN I FELT LIKE I WAS
BEING WATCHED AT THE SCHOOL

This was confirmed by a brand-new student
who was taking the IET© training from me. It was
during a lecture I was giving on the nine healing
Angels, naming them and describing what
cellular memory systems they govern and so
forth. She inquired as to whether or not I knew
there was a spirit watcher who was keeping an
eye on things here, and that he pops in and out
of the school. Instead of answering her, I asked
what he wanted. She said she would ask him. Her
answer was he told her do not worry about who
this is. It did not concern her. We both laughed
out loud. I do know she went on to say he is
someone who keeps an eye on things and takes
care of things as they are needed. I thanked my
student for the information, keeping the man I
had seen previously to myself. I thought it odd at
the time though I was not aware of his presence
in those exact moments and yet she was.

One night I decided to take the time to "delve
into" this spirit-man's energy. "Why are you
here? What do you want?" my mind asked.
Surrendering my energy and senses, trusting the
process, I waited for a response. Still no words

came. Knowing his energy was familiar to me somehow and "knowing" this was a wise being was all the information I could attain. I was hoping to establish some sort of communication with him which did not happen. My curiosity was getting the best of me. I made a mental note to ask about these happenings at the event I had coming up that week at my school.

CHANNELED MESSAGE AND THE ANGEL

The event was at the end of January. I had a channeler come to the school. This woman is known for channeling the Angels, The Mothers, and the Star Nations, ET's. I had met her years before and had been a client and fan of hers ever since. She does not go anywhere without asking her Guides first. She also asks who to channel for as the person would be feeling their energy. She called me back after speaking to her Guides to inform me with the good news the Angels wanted to come and she would be available. I was so thrilled to have the Angels channeled and invited twenty-nine people to experience this event.

When everyone was seated, and had asked all

their questions, guess what I did? Yes, you guessed it. My curiosity had gotten the best of me. I outed myself in front of twenty-nine people asking the Angel this woman was channeling, who was the tall man with bright white hair. The Angel's response was "Well, he wants you to know he is not as old as you think he is!" Oh wow, he was reading my mind. I had thought he was old and wise! The Angel laughed as if reading my thoughts, then said, "He will only say he is here for you and you are part of his lineage." The Angel continued saying, "He is here because you will be experiencing something so profound, that if you have any doubts at all you are a medium and healer, you will never doubt it again after this experience."

After this event, I spoke with the channeler and asked her when this would happen. She responded by telling me she saw the number "three" by March. It felt much sooner to me.

THREE DAYS LATER

Our son came off his life support and his heart stopped only three days later. That morning I woke with my heart aching to the point where I first questioned if I was having a heart attack. The next thing I did, of course, was to call and check on my son. There was no answer. I convinced myself he was in the shower to quiet the panic which was beginning to surface. I left him a voice message to call me when he had the chance. Forcing myself out the door and headed to the school for work.

The phone rang and I answered to the sound of frantic cries by my son's roommate, "Oh my God, Mrs. Finley he is dead!"

"NO!" I cried!

"I am so sorry we found him dead!"

"Dear God, please!!!" I cried.

His friend was obviously distraught. "It was awful, he was blue, was not breathing and he had no pulse or heartbeat! He was off his life support and his heart had stopped. Hurry get here now! Your mom called the rescue squad, and your daughter is doing CPR on him now!"

As I went to run and get my keys, it felt like something knocked my feet out from under me. I went to the ground. I was not hurt. I sat there for a moment while my students tried to comfort me as best as they could. One came over and reminded me to not to give up hope, because a miracle can happen. Another told me I had to pull myself together because my son was going to need me, reminding me how strong I am. I got up and went to get my keys again. My office door was locked! I could not get to my keys! I tried breaking the door down, then kicking it down as my students helplessly watched me.

Then I heard, "Ask one of them to take you." I asked, and one of them offered to take me. Ironically as she was driving, she followed the traffic laws. I know I would more than likely have driven recklessly, breaking the law. Perhaps this is why my keys ended up locked in the office.

My son's roommate called me back, "Mrs. Finley, your daughter got his heart started again. The rescue squad is working on him now. Hurry get here!"

I asked my student to please hurry, to please drive faster, and to please go through any red lights she could safely pass through. We arrived after what seemed like an eternity. My son was still upstairs. When I was able to touch him, he was ice cold, he was extremely grey, pale, and not responding. We followed the rescue squad to the trauma unit.

Another eternity seemed to pass as we waited helplessly for news. Occasionally I would ask to be let back there with him, only to be told no. "He has a rare syndrome," I said, only to be told they knew all about his syndrome. I remember my husband questioning how could they know all about his syndrome, when we had not told anyone what it is? The clerk responded she did not know how, only that they knew.

In the mix of all of this, I was making phone calls asking for my son to be put on prayer lists and asking my energy healing friends to work on him. Finally, feeling desperate, I went back to the clerk and told her she did not have any right to keep me from my son. He has a rare medical disability. He is unconscious and cannot speak for himself. If anything happened to him, she would regret it and so would the hospital. I told her I knew so and so, and she better not make me call them. Amazing how things happen when names are dropped. Within minutes, she called us back up there and let us go to the back to see our son.

The first thing I saw was a beautiful, young nurse crying, being consoled by her coworkers. I heard her mention my son by name through her sobs. Immediately I thought his heart had stopped again. I began to get hysterical once more. "Did his heart stop again? Is he dead?"

She looked at me and said, "No, his heart did not stop again," adding, "the doctors are working on him."

"Why are you crying then?" I asked, her eyes widened in shock momentarily.

"Mrs. Finley, I know it must be the trauma and that is why you do not recognize me." I stared back at her blankly. "You know me," she said, "I grew up with your kids, we used to play together. I am still friends with your daughter. I work here now in the trauma unit. When I saw him come into the unit, I told the doctors all about his rare syndrome."

DIVINE INTERVENTION

God, and his healing Angels were all around us on so many levels that day. Miracles happened. A miraculous string of "happen stances" led to his survival. Had my son not been called into work, I would have found him hours later, and he would have been gone several hours by that time. Not only that, before all this unfolded, the night before I called my mother to ask her to take him to work, my mother who also has the knowing, almost had the door where my son was staying broken down because she knew something was wrong and would not leave until my daughter called his roommate, to come home and let them in.

My daughter "coincidently" had finished a CPR class at my school a few days prior. When his roommate arrived back at the scene, she was able to get his heart started again. As I mentioned above, the nurse was a family friend and that is how the doctors all knew about his rare syndrome. When I called a friend of mine, in the midst of all this, she reminded me to start talking to those Angels I believed in so much!

ANGELIC MIRACLE

My son awoke from a coma with no residual affects after I laid my hands on him and channeled the IET® Healing Angel Energy. I whispered in his ear that I knew he did not believe in God and the Angels like I did, but I was going to ask them to heal him now. They had already tested for brain waves. The outcome did not look good.

Am I crazy to believe this was all part of the Divine's plan? No, I know I am not. I do know if his sister had not able to get his heart beating again, he would be gone. I also know he received excellent medical care in the trauma unit. However, I do believe the Healing Angels certainly did not hurt him in any way. The being from my lineage was right. This experience certainly helped to encourage me and affirmed I was on the right path to pursuing healing and mediumship. It also aged me one hundred years.

You will often hear me say I know it was not all about me. No doubt about that because if it were just about me, I would have never taken all those turns and detours. I feel my path was perfectly planned to lead me where I was best suited. Now I help to lead others to theirs. Perhaps I have given you some things to wonder about. Without any doubt or hesitation know this, we are all connected, we are never alone. We are being supported by those in Spirit, and the Angels.

I have learned to value the gifts God gave me without any fears, superstitions, or shame and I pray you will see the value in yourself. I have so many things to be grateful for in life. Life is nothing short of amazing. Do not dim the light of your soul.

"Spirit can only communicate with us
on our current level of understanding.
Our spiritual habits determine
what that level will be."
- Anthon St. Maarten

Mentoring Others

SOUL SISTER GROUP

Have you ever tried to talk to people who weren't like you, or who haven't ever experienced the things you have experienced? Believe me, I tried. I also knew how I sounded to the average non-sensitive, non-energy person. Quite frankly, to a person who has never had an experience or opened their mind to these possibilities we sound completely bonkers.

After selling the school, I started a Soul Sister Group with the intention of surrounding myself with like-minded women. Our group was called Soul Sisters because we all shared a healing heart and had the same desire to help others through healing. In my mind's eye, I had this vision of a group of women who would lift one another up, support one another, and cheer one another on in their endeavors.

Mentoring is wonderful support that makes a huge difference in the lives of people, including myself. When we have a safe environment to share in a non-judgmental way we grow and connect deeper.

Many of us felt we were not able to talk or connect in this way with our significant others, family, and "normal" friends. There were some who were able to, while the others could not, not even to their parents. Even though my husband and I are connected on a soul level and he respects and honors me, his mind works differently than mine. He is not on the same career path as me. He enjoys receiving an energy healing, and that is as far as he wants to go with it. I respect and honor him and his beliefs as well. This is what works for us.

It was a wonderful feeling to have others with similar visions, to talk to and share experiences with during their journey of what many considered "woo-woo" and all things weird. It was a place to find a listening ear, validation and support. When you are amongst those you can talk and be with, understood without judgement, no longer alone, and discover lifelong friendships, you have found your soul tribe.

Each time we met, I would lead them in a meditation, they would journal, and we had discussion. Afterwards, we would exchange energy healing by taking turns on the healing tables. This gave everyone in the group a chance to receive and give, sharing their healing abilities.

We were healers, massage therapists, energy practitioners of Reiki, which is a Japanese form of relaxation, where the practitioner acts as the medium for the universal god energy, Rei, combined with the life force energy Ki, to flow through them to their hands. The practitioner's hands are held slightly above or placed on the body during a treatment. Others practiced Angel Energy Healing, known as IET®. Integrated Energy Therapy®, integrated healing modality where the practitioner acts as the medium, treating points on the body, using the energy of the nine healing Angels to treat the body on a cellular memory level.

The soul sister group was more of a social, discussion and healing energy exchange group, verses a study group. Everyone would bring a snack to share, share our individual experiences. There was no charge for this. In addition to meeting monthly, I would host parties twice a year, once around the holidays, and the other another during the summer which was a pool party/sleep over with breakfast in the morning. We found community, support, and growth. We connected, finding good friends, and colleagues.

While keeping the monthly Soul Sister group going, I started a weekly gathering designed solely for psychic and mediumistic training. I included practice sessions for those interested. *The Spiritual Development Group* was born. Later, as a way to introduce new mediums to the public I started the *Meet the Mediums* platform.

This was all part of the Creator's divinely orchestrated plan, and my vision. My smile widened as I thought of how we were from all walks of life. We were ordinary women whom many of you may meet and interact with in everyday life. I could see their beautiful sparkly souls light up as they headed from their cars to my door.

They were happy to see each other, looking forward to the meditation, and exercises planned for the evening. In the beginning, the group was all women who were dedicated, intelligent women, career women, mothers, daughters, sisters, and wives. However, we are inclusive and welcomed men as well. The format was more of a learning environment, where I would give a short lecture, mentor, would practice, and learn to sharpen our psychic and mediumistic abilities.

When I think back to the very first Spiritual Development Circle, the memory warms my heart. I am so immensely proud of these individuals. I had been holding these weekly gathering in my home for the last several years, first with the Soul Sister group, and then with the Spiritual Development Group. I was suddenly reminded of how far they all have come since the beginning of their mentoring process.

Sharing what I had learned throughout the years with them, I was hoping to give them another perspective to think about. One important perspective to remember there is nothing to be afraid of when working as a medium. Being free of fear, being powerful, and being true to their authentic selves is how we should live our lives. I was reminding them they were already empowered.

For me, the religion of Spiritualism had helped me dispel many superstitions and fears. Once I embraced the religion and its beliefs, I had no more conflict within me as to where my abilities came from. I never had anxiety again where spirit was concerned, once it was explained to me how my body was reacting to the physical aspects of spirit's energy.

Each person who attended were psychics, and mediums. They simply had not remembered who they were while others had not ever acknowledged it. God knows it took me long enough! These men and women were intelligent, productive individuals. I was blown away with how diverse our group was, coming from all different fields with variety of educational backgrounds.

WHERE YOU WILL FIND MEDIUMS

You will find Mediums in every walk of life, in every ethnicity, among the rich and the poor. They come from many different spiritual backgrounds, and belief systems. They appear in the medical field, medical research, nurses, speech pathologist, special educational teachers, student aids to children with special needs. You find them working at colleges, others are retired police officers, lawyers, preschool teachers, some lack college degrees, and others have them. Others are stay at home moms, massage therapists, and energy practitioners. Still others are business owners, cosmetologists and salon owners, chemical engineers for hospitals, school bus drivers, young adults who were recovering addicts.

All of them are empathic, intuitive, sensitive, psychic, and mediumistic, and all of them had a knowing, or expressed that there was some piece of themselves missing, something feeling unfulfilled. All were looking to feed that part of themselves that was hungry so to speak. Each of them had a desire to improve themselves, and their lives. They were all seeking a relief from stress and anxiety.

What I offered to those that came to learn were opportunities of how to free and develop that part of themselves that they may have denied, dulled, shut down, or fought against. In a safe, non-judgmental learning environment. part of themselves which can become so polluted by so many things in our society, and by some of our life experiences of being judged and rejected. Many had not understood some of the things that were happening to them. Some of the things which pollute us most are things like superstitions, deep-seated, rigid, outdated religious beliefs, judgments, and fears.

UNDERSTANDING MEDIUMSHIP

What is a medium and how does mediumship work? A medium is an individual who is able to communicate with spirit in heaven. Mediums can communicate by establishing a link to spirit to the discarnate, meaning the person no longer has a body because they have passed on. This would include our pets too. This ability is based on the common belief our soul is eternal, and our spirits live on after we transition from here. A medium is the one who stands in between both worlds, bridging our physical world and the spirit world together. Some mediums refer to this ability as bridging.

Mediums receive information directly from the spirit. As a medium, I am aware of the presence of spirit. Often feeling as if there is a person there with me. Some mediums always work through spirit guides while others never do. Some only use their guides when needed. When I am overly tired, or sick I call upon my Guide to help me be of better service.

Spirit guides are special entities chosen by one's higher self that have a strong, life-long connection with the medium, who serves as their bridge into the spirit world

Depending on the individual and taking their life experiences into account, I do an assessment and recommend prerequisites if needed for beginners.

I feel it is a good idea for beginning Psychics and Mediums to have a basic understanding of the clairs, learn the basics of the human Chakra System, and the basics of the Human Energy Field, also known as the Aura. Another recommendation is to take psychic development courses, develop their symbol references and experience energy and how different energy feels.

Mediums have a natural awareness of those in the Spirit world who have passed over. We are the baby that waves to the unseen person, the infant who smiles, and coos to the air, or the small child who converses with a seemingly empty chair. Another example is recognizing someone who died before you were born in a photograph. As a small child these interactions are often so vivid most of us do not realize the person we are interacting with is a spirit until much later in life. Sometimes we find out after we are told, or when we look back over all those seeming coincidences, we now understand was an encounter with spirit.

WHAT IS THE DIFFERENCE BETWEEN MEDIUMS AND PSYCHICS?

Every medium is psychic and receives information from spirit through their psychic senses. It has been said that not every psychic is a medium. There is some truth to that statement, not every psychic is a medium. However, the mediumistic teaching worlds opinion on this has changed in recent years. Even I had been taught that not every psychic is a medium. Mediums are born. We now know that some psychics can certainly sense spirit but may not be able to link to spirit in order to communicate or sustain a link with the spiritual world for long. Psychic's home in on the human energy field, therefore they read your energy. In short psychic's perceive, whereas mediums receive. Mediums are the bridge, who link with those on the other side. Mediums are able to provide evidence and memories.

From spirit, (one who has passed on),
through spirit (the medium)
to spirit (their loved one here)

Most mediums can do everything a psychic can do. Mediums also have psychic senses. However, these abilities are used differently with Mediumship. Spirit will use the mediums psychic senses for the medium to better understand the messages they wish to communicate. It is important for the medium to remain linked and not go into their thinking minds.

Spirit will also use every experience the

medium has ever had to communicate their messages. For example, if the medium used to work in the medical field, or is well traveled, educated, or even speaks different languages, spirit will use this to impart a message. The mind of the medium is used in this manner to help them be a better communicator for spirit's messages.

When first starting out in the metaphysical field I worked mainly as a psychic. After taking courses in Tarot cards, astrology, the runes, and past lives, I found myself in the field as a professional reader.

Psychics can work exclusively with their abilities without using tools. Many psychics use some of the oracles mentioned above.

Psychic is a term used for anyone who has the ability to read the incarnate, meaning the living. This is not just for humans; psychics can also read animals. Psychics read their energy, or auras. Psychics can also read inanimate objects, through a technique known as Psychometry. Psychometry is the ability to read the imprints of energy from an object's history. Many psychics can sense spiritual energy or the imprints of spiritual energy. There are diverse types of psychic abilities.

Psychics use their psychic gifts, also known as "clairs" to read the energy of a person, place, or thing. In addition, they can also read the energies present on the earth and energies present within the universe. They can see the future and past. Many have predicted future events.

Psychic Senses are also known as "The Clairs." Both psychics and mediums use the clairs. Most mediums and psychics receive their information through the various combination of clairs listed below.

UNDERSTANDING THE CLAIRS

CLAIRVOYANCE which is clear seeing.

Clairvoyance is where one receives information from what they see in their mind's eye. Examples include, seeing flashes of light, colors, images, and symbols. Usually clairvoyants have wonderful imaginations. They can have visions of a future event, or vivid dreams, see subtle images, daydream like mini-movies, or see pictures in their mind.

This is one of my strongest psychic senses. However, I feel, know, and hear as well, as a psychic and medium. When working psychically, and I see a rose, I mention the little flower Saint Theresa. When I am working as a medium linked with spirit and they show me red, I know the spirit passed from an illness of the blood.

CLAIRSENTIENCE translates to clear feeling.

Clairsentience is often associated with one's gut feeling or intuition. This is also when you can experience or feel physical sensations. For example, you wake up to a deep ache in your heart, only to discover someone close was dying at the same time. At times I will feel waves of nausea when someone has died from stomach cancer.

As a medium, I have and can feel spirit's emotions. There are times I can be overcome with them because they are so strong. In the beginning of my mediumship, it was difficult for me to keep my composure. If I remind myself what I am feeling does not belong to me and belongs to spirit, it helps me to go on to hold the link to deliver the evidence and messages.

CLAIREMPATHY is clear emotion.

Some say this is a component of clairsentience. Clairempathy is the ability to sense or perceive the emotions of others. An example is, you walk into the room where people appear to be fine and sense an argument had previously taken place. Another example is when you feel something is bothering someone who is putting on a happy face.

As a medium, I will feel a physical sensation, which tells me how a spirit died. This happens quickly and has not ever stayed with me.

CLAIRCOGNIZANCE which is clear knowing.

Claircognizance is the ability to know things consistently without any other explanation or doubt. It can feel like a gut feeling, one you cannot explain. It is having the gift of knowing the truth. Examples of claircognizance are, she always knew she was going to be a doctor, even though she hated taking medicine, or I knew the person was not being truthful. It is knowing when your friends or partner is bad news, or someone is being abused.

As a medium when in the presence of a spirit, you will hear me say, "...and I know this man was a writer, as surely as I know I am standing here." You know because of the deep feeling within, it is an unshakable feeling.

CLAIRAUDIENCE simply put is clear hearing.

Clairaudience is usually heard inside your head, never mean or heard in a detrimental way. In other words, the voice will never tell you to harm someone or yourself. You may hear noises, music, or words. An example would be a thought suddenly drops into your head and sounds like your voice. You know it is not your voice especially because it has an accent. Mediums can sometimes hear the voice of their guide. Clairaudience can also be a voice you hear sounding like it is coming from up above, or outside of yourself. These experiences are almost always a warning. For example, being told suddenly to move or run.

Clients we are reading for have reported feeling

the strong presence of their loved one as well. This is usually enough evidence for them, as they feel the soul to soul connection. More than a few have told me the presence of their loved one was so clearly felt, they forgot it was me delivering the messages. What a wonderful and beautiful compliment.

CLAIROLFACTION or CLAIRALIENCE is clear smelling.

Clear smelling is the ability to smell odors and/or things. An example would be smelling the scent of roses in the dead of winter when the grounds are covered with snow. Another could be smelling your dad's after shave, or your grandmother's favorite flower.

As a medium, I can smell coffee or Italian gravy when they are spirit's favorite things. Smelling is an interesting clair for me, as it is usually coupled with clairgustance.

CLAIRGUSTANCE is clear taste.

Clear taste is the ability to taste something you

have not eaten or drank, yet you can taste in your mouth. When Spirit has been swimming with sea turtles, I have tasted the salt water and even have smelled the salt in the air. This was and is an amazing experience for me when practicing as a medium. When I have gotten a metallic taste in my mouth, I now know the spirit had lots of medication, and possibly an addiction to medicines used for pain. I have even tasted oranges when spirit loved them. The downside of Clairgustance is when you taste something you do not like or care for.

MEDIUMSHIP MODALITIES

When training psychics and mediums on a beginning level, I have them bring a journal. This is used for the development of what I call their Symbol Pictionary Reference. During training, we devote a set amount of time where I give them a symbol and intuitively write what the symbols represent to them. When not in class, as part of their commitment to development, the students are required to continue to add to this journal of references. This exercise is followed up a few weeks later, by a practice exchange session with one another. In these exercises, they try out their intuitive symbols for accuracy.

Most mediumship today is known as mental mediumship, meaning it is a faculty of the mind. This can be subdivided into communicating and healing mediumship. Simply put, Mental Mediumship is a form of communication between the medium and the spirit through their mind, a mind to mind connection.

Some mediums may hear words or have an automatic knowing. Others may feel the emotions connected to spirit, or even feel a physical symptom. For others, they have a knowing, or see pictures, spirit, colors, memories and much more.

For the beginner Mediums, together we develop a system they can use to help them learn to begin to communicate with spirit. This system is a sample to help them determine things about spirit (also called the communicator):

- Are they a man or a woman?
- Were they young or were they old?
- What did they look like?
  - Short
  - Tall

- Balding
- Thin build
- Thicker build

Who are they in relation to the sitter (the one receiving the messages):

- Grandparent
- Parent
- Sibling
- Cousin
- Spouse
- Friend
- Neighbor

Continue to converse, get to know them better:

- How old were they when they passed?
- What ailments did they have if any?
- How did they die?
- What did they do for a living?
- What are their favorite memories?

TRANCE MEDIUMSHIP

There are various levels of trance mediumship. Light to deep, with each level the medium is always present and in control. The lightest being when the trance medium enters into an altered state to entrance with spirit and from there communicating with Spirit, delivering their messages. This is still mental mediumship; however, it is a soul to soul experience. The medium invites spirit to entrance with them and is always present and in control.

Trance is more of an experience. When I use trance mediumship, I invite the spirit to entrance with me. Through the process of surrendering and allowing my mind and body to become a vessel for the spirit to be able to communicate, I connect my soul to spirit's soul. If I am entrancing with healing beings, I use trance to enhance the healing experience.

Personally, this has been an amazing experience for me. More than once I have had the blessings of entrancing with Healing Beings from the Place of Light. Allowing my body to be used as a vessel for healing beings, healing energy, my mind is with them, aware and calm. Through practice, and dedication, during trance mediumship when facilitating a healing, I have experienced times where my mind is able to receive and give messages from those in the spirit world, while simultaneously entranced by beings from the place of light giving healing energy to the participants through me.

Sometimes manifestations may occur when one is using trance. For example, transmutation often occurs where onlookers have seen different faces overshadowing the trance mediums. Sometimes spirit will use their voice box to manifest speaking and give messages.

During mediumistic spiritual healing, the link is established with the Creator, or to the Spirit world healing spirits, and is channeled through the medium. This is similar to trance mediumship.

SPIRITUAL HEALING

When practicing pure spiritual healing, you are the vessel for the God energy, and do not mix messages with the healing. Spirit will often show up; however, the healer gives an energetic nod of acknowledgement and does not engage in communication. The reason for this, you are remaining fully present and a clear vessel. The flow of energy is not interrupted in any way. There is also Spiritual Healing done within Spiritual Churches as shared above. Again, the medium is the vessel in which the healing energies are delivered to the sitter.

IMPORTANT REMINDERS BEFORE HEALING

Before the session starts, the healer asks permission to touch the individual gently upon their shoulders, and again asks permission to provide the healing. This is ethical, sets a high standard and shows professionalism of the healer.

There are other forms of Mediumship you may now be inspired to investigate.

TRAINING TOOLS

I use meditation as one way to attune students to the energy of spirit and to help the students develop. I have included for you a sample of what is provided to them. Every meditation I lead is different and inspired by spirit for each group of students.

There are other tools I use in addition to meditation and sitting in the silence discipline. These tools are designed to further develop the practice of focusing the mind for the developing student. They can use these or use anything which requires focus.

One exercise I love is listening to music and only focusing on one instrument. After the music piece is finished, I have the students focus on the one instrument and then have them add another. Listening for a single instrument in a piece of music is certainly an exercise of focus. Another is using color, where you focus on a single color for a timed period. I have the students set a timer for thirty seconds and ask them to continue building up their focused time. Then have them select another color.

WHITE LIGHT/SITTING IN THE SILENCE/ HEALING MEDITATION

This is the Meditation I mentioned earlier which is used in my development circles.

TAKE NOTE:
You can use this as written, make three different meditations, or use pieces of this and that. This is for your personal use. I suggest recording this and play it back later for yourself.

Many people have given me wonderful feedback after they have experienced it. Sometimes individuals may feel inspired to add relaxation music in the background. If you are using this to sit in the silence, I would recommend not using music. I like to quiet my mind, and this has helped me distinguish my thoughts from spirits.

SOME DIRECTION

When you are recording for your personal use, speak in an even tone, slow and steady calm voice. The (....) are placed to help you know when to pause. Remember to breathe and take your time. Enjoy!

Sit as straight as possible. If your head begins to move forward or to the side, imagine there is a fine golden thread running through your spine, connecting straight up to your crown which will help to straighten and keep your posture aligned.

THE MEDITATION BEGINS

Breathe in through your nose, holding the breath to the mental count of four. Slowly exhale through your mouth. On the inhale, you can imagine you are breathing in peace, and on the exhale, imagine letting go of anything which no longer serves you. With each breath you take, you find yourself becoming more and more relaxed. So deeply relaxed, you find your muscles softening, relaxing, deeply relaxing....

If you find your mind beginning to wander, know that is perfectly normal. Bring your focus back again to your breath.... Breathing in and out.... focus on your breathing, all the while with each and every breath you are taking, you are becoming more deeply relaxed.... with each and every breath you are taking, you are feeling more and more relaxed.... Your muscles softening as they are releasing any tension, any stress they may be holding.... as you breathe in.... and out.... In.... and out.... you are finding your body to be so very relaxed.... and your breathing naturally.... in a natural rhythm.... continue to breathe.... and as you do.... you are aware of how good you feel as you notice a peaceful feeling begins to unfold and spread throughout your body.... from the top of your head to the tips of your toes.... You are feeling peaceful and so very relaxed.... continue to breathe and as you do, you are becoming more and more relaxed.... with and every breath you deeply relax.... letting go and enjoying the feelings of peace....

Bring your attention now to the weight of your body. Be aware of the weight of your body.... Continue to Breathe.... taking deep breaths as you need them.... until you find yourself breathing normally in and out.... in and out....

Bring your attention to the top of your head.... your crown chakra now.... once there, imagine the top of your crown chakra. There is an abundance of beautiful white light that has accumulated.... this beautiful white light has an intelligence of the creator God.... it is also healing....cleansing.... Imagine now your crown chakra is opening, just like a flower opens to accept the sun's nourishment.... when you are ready, open the crown chakra. Invite the beautiful white light to pour down into it.... as if it were a liquid light.... as you let the light pour into the top of your crown chakra.... know the white light cleanses and clears the area, as the light pours down it does so to the rhythm of your breathing and begins filling your head completely.... and as it does, the light touches your third eye.... the front, back, and sides of your head, your face, and ears. The light continues pouring down into your neck, the front and back of your neck, touching your throat chakra.... imagine the light is spreading through the front, sides and back of your neck, and spilling down over your shoulders, down your arms, all the way down to your wrist, to your hands and to your fingertips.... The light is spreading down into all the areas of your torso, filling each and every cell as it does so.... The light fills your heart center, fills your belly, your pelvic area, your hips, thighs, knees, your calves, ankles, feet and toes. The light pours into you completely, until every cell of your body is completely saturated with the light.... Your physical body is completely filled, radiating with this light and you are feeling so deeply relaxed, so peaceful, keenly aware of the peaceful feelings the light brings with it.

Feel the peace the white light brings with it, become aware of how bright and light and subtle your physical body has become.... Imagine now this light moves past your physical body, going out past your skin, forming into a bubble that is surrounding you now.... it is as if you could move upwards and away from your physical body within this bubble.... and into that higher part of your mind.... your soul self, one now with the creator God. This is where you will find clarity and you will know all is well.

Be at peace with yourself and know in this state of being, you are still, quiet.... your mind is peaceful and contented.... from this place.... send signals to your body.... from this higher state of mind, by using that quiet inner voice which connects the lower and higher minds.... send positive signals of peace and contentment to your mind, body and spirit.... now, you have clarity and no fear.... you know all the negativity and fears that your body and mind has held onto for so very long are being saturated by the light.... in this place, they are transmuted into healthy loving energy by the light.... let go of the illusion of separation.... let it go.... for fear is false energies appearing real.... and allow the divine white light and higher self-replace these lower energies with the knowingness you are safe, you are powerful.... with each and every breath you are again filled with this knowledge from the divine, you are filled with the intelligence and wisdom which the light brings with it....

From this higher state of mind, send down signals to your body that all is well, knowing you have the ability to be still, even though things around you are in motion. The ability to be calm in the face of all and any adversity. Know you can tap into this higher state of self, and into what we may know as our psychic senses. Know this is one of the creator God's many gifts to us.... Take some time to enjoy this elevated state of mind, sit a while in the power.... sit awhile in the silence of your mind, enjoying, being one with the creator.... and yourself and recognize how good it feels.............................

Know that all through you and around you, you are radiating beautiful white light.... your soul is sparkling, shining, radiating.... know as you chose to shine your light, within, and outside of yourself, know this light is where you come from. You are a spark of that divinity, that intelligence, the all-knowing and powerful.... know you can call upon it and it will always burst forth like a ginormous starburst, sending healing energy into yourself, to others, to other places.... the white light heals any residual negative energy within you or cleansing the energies outside of you.... let go, surrender.... allow the light to heal old scars, old memories and any residual energies which no longer serve your highest purpose, feel the white light begin to move upward and as it does it rights, and heals in all times.... allow the light to go through you now, and as it moves upward feel it bringing peace throughout yourself. Feel the balance.... as the white light is traveling upward, it again touches the top of your head.... and travels out of your crown chakra and you begin to feel reconnected again to the creator, and to the higher part of yourself that connects you to all things.... feel how your body has accepted the relaxation, peace and contentment. Feel the weight of your body in this relaxed state.... it's as if its weightless, and grounded at the same time, you find yourself being present in your body, and your mind is awakened, filled with peace and contentment and the energy of the creator God.

Begin to breathe more deeply now.... with each and every breath you take, you are now slowly coming back into your physical body.... coming back now.... taking nice deep breaths, filling your lungs and body with these breaths, begin to bring your attention to your eyes, bring your awareness to your hands and feet now. Begin moving your hands and feet around, as you do so become aware of your eyes again.... when you are ready open your eyes.... Open your eyes now.

INSTRUCTIONS

Afterward, take some time to write about your experience.

- Observe how you feel.
- Journal your thoughts.
- Write down messages.

HEALING MESSAGES

How do I help those who seek me out? One of the most common ways, we as mediums are able to aid those who seek us out is to deliver messages that are evidential. We share the memories from when the spirit person was alive, and even current situations where their loved ones participated in, from spirit while they were in heaven.

This is another example of proof; spirits still see and participate in our lives. There is also Spiritual Healing. Another way to help is through mentoring people who are like myself. I am devoted to helping them better understand themselves, to handle fears, misconceptions, or superstitions they may struggle with. I provide them with spiritual tools and supervised practice so they could develop their gifts and abilities if they chose to do so.

I believe within the heart of a true medium lies a *compassionate healer*. Personally, for me, even though I was born as a natural medium, the Creator knew when my soul would be ready. I was called back to mediumship. I was told I was needed and why. I was asked to be of service when my soul was ready. Of my own free will, I choose to be of service to those in Spirit. Although I cannot take their loved one's grief away, I may be able to help them move along in their grieving process.

The messages delivered can be healing themselves, especially if they are given in an ethical, compassionate and responsible way. It is important not to retraumatize anyone we sit for. Balancing the heartfelt message along with providing the evidence to those who seek us out, we the medium, provide proof of the eternal soul. In some instances, we give hope to those left here to grieve, or to those who may have had none.

There will always be those who are skeptics regarding this. Some individuals do not believe in an afterlife and then there are those who have strong religious beliefs who worry about their loved one's soul and wellbeing.

MENTORING OTHERS LIKE MYSELF

A question I often ask my students to help identify if they may be a medium is "Who has had issues with anxiety or fearful feelings". I follow that question up, with others specific to identifying Mediumistic abilities. This helps them realize they are not alone. Helping them to feel more confident when raising their own hands. It is a good thing. I knew full well what many of them were experiencing. I lived it.

It is important to explain why they may have been experiencing these things. This clears a pathway to learn ways to develop their abilities or, at the very least, provides them ways to honor that part of themselves.

Depending on the individual and taking their life experiences into account, I do an assessment and recommend a prerequisite class if needed for beginners. I feel it is a good idea for beginning Psychics and Mediums to have a basic understanding of the clairs and for them to learn the basics of the human Chakra System, and the basics of the Human Energy Field, also known as the Aura. It is a good idea to take psychic development courses, develop their symbol references, and to have them experience energy and how different energy feels. I offer training and so do others. James Van Praagh has many different development courses as well.

Mediums can receive information directly from the spirit. Some mediums always work through spirit guides while others never work through a spiritual guide. Still others only use their guides when needed. When I am overly tired, or sick I call upon my Guide to help me be of service. Spirit guides are special entities chosen by the higher self that have a strong, life-long connection with the medium, who serve as their bridge into the spirit world. One of the meditations we would use in class is the Chakra Visualization and teaching provided below.

UNDERSTANDING THE BASIC CHAKRAS

There are many chakras throughout the body. A basic understanding is needed at this point. Briefly, I will share the most basic information of the Seven main chakras. What is a chakra? A chakra is a wheel shaped vortex of spinning energy. They are in constant motion and are located along your vertebrae, known as your spinal column. The colors associated with each chakra can also be found in a rainbow. Listed are the names and colors associated with each one and approximate location on the human body.

1. ROOT CHAKRA (Red Color)
    Location: tailbone area, at the base of your spine

2. Sacral Chakra (Orange Color)
    Location: Lower abdomen, two inches below belly button

3. Solar Plexus Chakra (Yellow Color)
    Location: Upper abdomen, stomach area

4. Heart Chakra (Green Color)
    Location: Just above the heart, center of chest

5. Throat Chakra (Blue Color)
    Location: voice box area, throat

6. Third Eye Chakra (Indigo Color)
    Location: along the brow line, between your eyes

7. The Crown Chakra (Violet Color)
    Location: on top of your head

All seven chakras govern various organs and glands within the body. Each chakra closely coincides with Western medicine as far as location and governing function. The chakras are in the same area as the ganglions plexus of the peripheral nervous system where the nerves branch off to supply and nourish the organs and glands. This information brought eastern philosophy together with western medicine for me. These chakras are responsible for disturbing the life energy, known as Qi or Prana.

The first chakra is referred to as the base chakra and begins at the base of the spine These spinning energy vortex centers are vital to an individual and their overall state of wellbeing. Eastern medicine believes disease is caused when our life force is low. These seven chakras are also used in the energy healing modality called Reiki. If you are a Reiki Practitioner, you are already practicing a form of Mediumship. Just saying.

Both Psychics and Mediums use these centers along with their clairs to process information. Specifically, with Mediumship, when these centers are opened and expanded, it is believed this helps to increase and sustain the link and the medium's power. Therefore, strengthening your connection to the spirt world allows the flow of information to be processed through the medium.

There are disciplines developing psychic and mediums can use one to two times per week designed to open and expand these centers. This is an excellent idea considering we need to keep ourselves open and willing to be a better conduit receiver of information from the spirit world. I would recommend further study of the chakra system, the human aura and the clairs as part of your development.

CHAKRA MEDITATION

There are many meditations available for individuals to choose from, should you not want to read and record these examples. Each meditation I lead is different and always inspired by spirit. This Chakra Meditation was channeled by me for this book. It is a short visualization you can use to open, clear, and expand your chakras:

After taking several deep, relaxing breaths to relax yourself. Imagine yourself sprouting roots from the bottom of your feet and follow those roots as they travel downward to where they meet core mother earth. Now, imagine those roots wrapping securely around core mother earth.... grounding you. Ask mother earth to send her light upward through these roots imagining the light traveling upward, super charging the roots.... see and feel the energy move all the way up through the bottoms of your feet. Now, imagine this light continuing its journey upward, touching your root chakra. As it touches this center it sparks, igniting the root center, opening and expanding your root chakra.... imagine this light is continuing to travel upward, bringing with it the light of the root chakra, until it meets your sacral chakra. Sparking, igniting, and expanding your sacral chakra, it travels upward. The light goes up and as it does, it brings the light of the chakras before it as it meets your solar plexus. It sparks, igniting the divinity within you, and you remember who you are.... opening and expanding the solar plexus. The light continues onward and upward, bringing the light of the prior chakras with it, meeting your heart center, where it again sparks, igniting, opening, and expanding the heart center. As it does so, it fills the center with the energy of compassion, opening your heart in compassion, not only for others, but for yourself as well. Your heart center expands and the light travels upward, where it meets your throat chakra, sparking, igniting, opening, and expanding the throat center, continuing its upward travel. Again, it sparks, ignites, opens, and expands your third eye chakra, further charging this center with the light, moving upward where it finally meets your crown chakra. Once more it sparks, ignites, opens, and expands your crown center. Now, breathe deeply and feel your energy centers charged, open, and expanded.

When you are finished with this visualization, remember to put your chakras or energy centers back into their normal functioning vibration.

How to put your chakra system back into its normal functioning vibration: Your higher self has an innate knowing of how energy follows intention. This is done with intention. Simply intend for your chakras to go back to their normal functioning vibration by saying:

I now ask my root center to go back to its normal functioning vibration

I now ask my sacrum center to go back to its normal functioning vibration

I now ask my solar plexus center to go back to its normal functioning vibration

I now ask my heart center to go back to its normal functioning vibration

I now ask my throat center to go back to its normal functioning vibration

I now ask my third eye center to go back to its normal functioning vibration

I now ask my crown center to go back to its normal functioning vibration

"Sometimes Angels
sing to you in the wind,
all you have to do
is listen."

Part
Four

Readings
and Hope

Spirits are energy.
Nature and electricity
become their vocal cords.
Coincidence and dreams
become their language.
- Silvia Rossi

Sharing the Gift ~ Readings

Readings/channelings of actual clients, names have been changed to protect their privacy.

#1: A LITTLE BIT OF HEAVEN

When working as a Psychic Card Reader, my Mediumship emerged rather naturally. I was giving a card reading to a young woman. All the sudden, I had a knowing someone close to her had passed in an automobile accident. I could smell perfume, it was lemony. I commented how I smelled a lemony perfume. I asked the young lady if she was wearing lemony perfume? "No, but it means something to me," she answered.

Smelling the pleasant lemony fragrance, and smiling to myself, I felt the presence of spirit. I became aware of a young female spirit who looked to be about sixteen.

I was with her when the dentist removed her braces. We went for ice cream with gooey caramel topping afterwards. Tell her, ask her if she remembers.

The young lady I was reading for was petite with a friendly smile. She had introduced herself as Maria. As soon as she sat down, the spirit of the young woman was waving at me. Hi, I am Rita, she was a wonderful communicator.

"Rita is here, and she asked me to ask you if you remember the ice cream with caramel after getting your braces off."

"Yes," she smiled, "I remember."

Right off she let me know how she regretted dying on Mother's Day. Ask her to please let my mom know I love her, Daddy, and Brian, and I am okay. Every Mother's Day I am going to send her sunflowers please tell her she asked my sitter.

I mentioned her age, what she looked like as well to this pretty young woman sitting across from me. Providing the evidence, this was another car accident. Rita, the spirit she wanted to apologize to the family and please let Mom know she came through. I am so, so sorry I really screwed up. Rita explained she did not remember the accident. She showed me a scene in my mind of all of them (friends). They were riding in the car, enjoying going up and down the hills. I could hear their laughter as she made me aware. They were laughing and listening to the music. The song, *"Born in the USA"* came to me when I mentioned this Rita was doing a head bang and playing an imaginary guitar. The client broke out in a huge smile confirming her cousin loved that song!
I mentioned there was a strong chemical smell assaulting my nose. I could smell it. Rita's cousin nodded her head. "Yes," saying she understood that.

Going on, she gave me a flying feeling. I told her cousin, "I know she lost control of the car."

Nodding again "Yes, she was driving," she said.

The next thing she showed me was that she

185

was with a beautiful Angel standing with her looking back at the crash site. There were other Angels sent to the others she told me. The Angel took me to our grandmother who was waiting for me in Heaven. Heaven is beautiful, I am so happy here.

Please tell Mom I am so sorry this certainly was not what I intended to happen. I love you all.

The young lady promised to get the message to the rest of the family. The facts I provided gave evidence as well. For example, I knew the number of people in the car, how one survived and one had a child here still. Knowing she did not suffer, and the Angels and their family were there to greet them made all the difference to this family. The client also shared with me after the reading, the surviving friend swore an Angel pulled him from the wreck and stayed with him until help arrived.

#2: I BLAMED MYSELF

I read for a gentleman, who had come to see me on a recommendation from a family friend whose judgement he trusted. He looked to be in

his forties. He no sooner sat down and introduced himself as Tony, when I was made aware of a spirit of a woman, who looked to be in her late sixties, seventy at the most. I conveyed all this to him. Immediately I felt a tightness in the chest and faint. "I have a woman here who had a bad heart, she makes me feel as though she is your mom."
I know she did not die because of it.

"Yes," he answered.

Elenore, my name is Elenore. I am his mom, and I passed in car accident, she said. Her spirit eyes looking lovingly at him, she prompted me to look at him. I feel so bad for him. She wanted him to know she was with Timmy. She died instantly.

"She is with Timmy." Now this client was visibly grief stricken, his eyes welling up with tears. He was reaching for the box of tissues I kept within reach.

"Oh, thank God she has him," he was visibly relieved. As if on cue, his mother reached her hand out behind her and then she had a young man by the hand, both now were in my presence. I had an awareness of head trauma. Timmy made me aware he had passed in the same automobile accident.

"Timmy wants me to tell you." Tell him I knew my uncle was there, and he mentions his uncle was there and he was a hero and did everything he could. This lovely father was crying freely now and thanking me. Tell him I had fallen to sleep on the way home, he knows I did. I am alright, I did not even see or feel the impact when the truck hit us. My other Grammy came to greet us.

My client was overcome with emotion. I asked him if he wanted to take a break, he shook his head no. He started to say something about Timmy's uncle and I stopped him, giving him time to catch his breath. I switched my attention to see if the uncle was there and if I could connect to him.

"He was not there with spirit," I told my client.

"No, he would not be, he is alive."

I asked; "You would understand he was there though?"

"Yes, I do. Timmy was found unconscious at the scene; my brother was the paramedic called to the scene, he worked on him. My son never woke up."

I could feel both his mother and son close I started to repeat their message. They were asking me to tell him to forgive yourself, and they want you to know they were together and asked he forgive the person who caused the accident. They had concerns about his wellbeing as well. I let him know. His son was adorable. He showed me his football jersey colors and number on the shirt. Tell Dad about my football jersey and give him my number 22. Tell Mommy and my sissy I still see and hear them, grandmom does too. I love you all so much. I am alright and tell Mommy hello from Grammy. I love you son; we are all alright and I do not want to see you on this side anytime soon. With that he smiled a genuine smile.

After the reading this client confirmed the information. He could not thank me enough for the messages. He was driving and blamed himself for not seeing the oncoming truck. Rationally, he knew the truck blew the light, T-boning the passenger side. No one blamed him but himself. He was working on forgiving the driver who had a seizure and was also unconscious at the time of the accident. He expressed there was no doubt this was his mother and son. The uncle was one of the paramedics who answered the call. His son played football and the number was correct. He confirmed he was driving and was clinically depressed. I handed him the name of a group that helped my family members after their child died.

#3: MINI ME AND FAMILY

I read for a woman named Carmella, she was adorable. She had a sadness about her even though she was smartly dressed in boots and a miniskirt. She had bobbed shiny black hair and beautiful green eyes which reflected her sadness.

"Hello," I introduced myself to her and invited her to sit down. She told me right off she did not believe in life after death much less what I did. I thought, okay, then why are you here?

She is here because of me, I heard behind me. I turned to see a spirit of her mini-me standing there. Oh, hello, I thought. Who are you? I am me. I had nonchalantly turned back around and was struck with knowing this was important.

This little toddler, who showed me she was this many (three) was so happy her mommy was there, wanted me to let her mommy know she did not neglect her, she had died because of the medical error. My mommy tried to tell the doctors to clean out my drain, but they would not listen. Mommy was singing the sunshine song to me when I went to sleep and never woke up. She was giggling.
I have been playing with mommy's shoes and the TV when she is trying to read. I make it loud. I am playing with the other kids here and am with her friend Jen.

I thought, well, I better get this reading going. I relayed all of what her little daughter was telling me. I was not sure if mom was in shock, as it appeared, she was barely breathing.

I asked, "Would you understand a little girl of about three who passed away recently?"

She stared straight at me not blinking, there was no response. As a mother myself, my heart went out to her. I felt her grief. I acted like she answered me and went on at her little girl's urging.

"I have a little girl here who looks just like you. She wanted to let you know she has been moving your shoes and making the television sound blast when you are trying to read in the evenings." I heard the woman sob and continued. "She is so happy to see you and has been trying to get you here for weeks. She said her name was Me and that you were singing the sunshine song to her when she went to sleep."

"It is true! Oh my God!" Carmella was shocked, I had the chills as I was listening to her talk through her tears. She was saying almost to herself, this must be her. "I did not tell anyone about the song and singing to her when she died."

Her little girl "Me" was nudging me. She said you need to know, she is asking me to tell her mommy, this was not her fault. She tried to tell the doctors to clean out my drain, but they would not listen. You did not do anything wrong! Mommy you are drinking too much with your medicine. Stop it, I want you to stop it! That is why I knocked over the picture on the night table, she explained.

This little one was spirited. I am with Aunt Jen

and playing, "She is with a Jen."

"Thank you. I am glad she is with Jen. She was my friend. My kids all called her Aunt Jen." Carmella was barely able to contain her happiness. She asked me to tell her little girl she loved her so much.

I explained she can hear you and talk to her anytime. She promised to stop drinking and continue with therapy. She also told me I made a believer out of her. I quickly explained her brilliant little Mini-Me gets all the credit, not me.

"I am so glad I came," she told me. This was the first time since her daughter had died, she felt hope. She confirmed the hospital tried to make her out to be neglectful after her daughter had died. The autopsy showed a blockage in her shunt just like Mom suspected. It was a simple fix, she tried to tell them this happened before to her little one and she had the same symptoms. She had a lawsuit as well. This client and I would run into each other at a department store years later. She made it a point to come over to me and thank me for the reading all those years before. She claimed hearing proof of her daughter's soul's survival helped her more than any medicine could.

I am so grateful and humbled with each reading. I do not need any thanks; it is my honor.

I often encourage families to keep those special traditions going their loved ones liked during those special occasions and holidays. I encourage them to still talk to them and about them with family and loved ones. Sharing the happiest of times and laughter helps honor them.

Messages and Thanks

THE COMPASSIONATE HEART AND A MESSAGE FROM THE ANGELS

I was writing this part on the compassionate heart and WAS INSPIRED to ask the angels to channel a message through me for the book. They addressed their view on evil. I included what I wrote after discerning upon their message in relation to mediumship.

I begin every day with a prayer of gratitude and end everyday in gratitude. I pray and send healing as part of my daily regimen. When I pray or send healing I do so by opening my heart in unconditional love and compassion for others.

I have also learned the importance of opening my heart in these energies for myself as well. It is the same when I am doing Mediumship.

Compassion for me is understanding the suffering of others. It is non-judgmental, and unconditional love of the self and others. I still seek ways to improve myself. I make an effort to always be a good and kind person.

My life has taught me how to live in the energy of compassion. I have been a caregiver, and I have been the one in need of care. I remember many times where my heart went out to those were suffering. In those times when I needed a reminder, I found myself given a lesson through a circumstance. One I either lived through to help give me a better understand or one I witnessed.

How can we become more compassionate? By paying attention to our feelings and to how we make others feel. Be observant. Open our hearts. One way is being of service to others.

So many people were good to me throughout my life, and to my family in those days when we were struggling, and on so many levels. Acts of kindness are free. I wanted to give back, so I joined the Lioness Club, which is derived from our local Lions Club. All the Lion/Lioness are part of the International Lions organization. We raise funds for those less fortunate in our communities. We give to the blind, deaf, our serve men and women. We give to the hungry and the sick. Compassion creates understanding.

You know those times where you may have had a parent, or grandparent, or even a friend who asks you to listen to them because they lived it and know better? They have the understanding because they lived and experienced it. That is how compassion is. Compassion is caring, loving, kind. Compassion is empathy, giving us the gift of understanding. So, we can empathize, and feel what another is going through. I pray this helps me be a better voice for those in the spirit world.

Compassion is also supporting another. Giving another a helping hand up verses kicking them when they are down or knocking them down when they are up. This is true Power. Our loved ones in heaven see and hear us, and know what we are going through. They come to you through the medium with compassion, and messages of encouragement.

When they come through, they present with the same personality, mannerisms so we can recognize them. I have never had an evil spirit come near me. Even if they were a horrible hurtful human, and they come through, it is usually to apologize, and/or ask for forgiveness. They do so to make amends, for the betterment of their souls in addition to yours. You see we are given the chance to grow and evolve on the other side as well.

The Compassionate Heart of a Medium is part of the healing we do as Mediums. I take the time with every session and gallery demonstration to educate. Why? To help clear up any fears or fallacies one may have of mediumship. To shine the light of hope where there is none. There is much pressure to conform. Years ago, this only happened within our religious realms or through an individual's choice of religion. These days it is being done throughout our society. Anything from our choice of politics, to the color of our skin, can be a way for some to worm their way in to continue to cause doubts, spread fear to divide us. This is not the Angels or the Creator's way. To those who experience the ramifications of this division, know this our Creator and His Angels are working on it and we need to do our part.

Do not let anything dim your light!

CHANNELED BY DEBORAH FINLEY; FROM THE ANGELS: 7-11-2020

Dear Ones, thank you, we come to you with a compassionate heart and message of love. We are here for you. When you are ready to invite us into your life, know we rejoice to work on the behalf of your highest good and for the benefit of all humankind.

There are many things that are good in your world. Many of you see this and are grateful, joyful, loving and giving, even though challenged by the current times. There are also those things that are out of balance and upsetting to us as they are to you. Do not lose hope dear ones! We see the challenges and negative being dwelled upon and highlighted. It is as if many of you are being bombarded with this negativity whenever the opportunity presents itself. Do not let this beat you down and fill your heart with disease. Focus on all that is good.

We were created to help you, yet many of us sit and wait, wanting to make a difference in helping you all achieve heaven on earth. All who seek this know it is possible. Know you are loved and protected.

Many who see beyond the veil see beyond the illusions. We the Angels are here to assist you in lifting the illusion of helplessness, of hopelessness energies. Look within, to your higher self which is infinitely connected to the God source and knows the truth. Much disruption comes from the lower vibration. The lower vibration which is seeking now more than ever to increase this chaos.

You are curious on our views of Evil. Those who humans have named are different and worse. Those different ones including those who do not agree or go along with the masses, are being bullied, branded, and sometimes viciously destroyed. This the Angels see and know is a form of EVIL. Many humans know, Evil is and has always been 'human made'. Which creates an illusion of feeling oh so powerful, but only for the truly weakened ones. This is not how to be powerful in its true sense. It saddens us as it does many of you, that in this sense not much has changed throughout your society, just the avenues by which this is being done to people.

Many of you are asking us what are you to do? Dear ones, be joyful, because this is what God wants for you, keep on doing your work for the highest good of all! We the Angels will help you, giving you the strength to stand strong and confident in who you are. Filling and supporting you in the days ahead, and always. You are never alone! We Angels know true power is NEVER found at the expense of another.

In this time and in all time, call upon our creator and his Angels. We the Angels shall continue to assist you. Do not live in fear, or close your hearts to love, open them in compassion. Open your hearts in the energy of unconditional love of your creator, this is the Gateway to Understanding.

We say to the lightworkers, and to all the children of the Creator, we implore you to remember who you are! True strength is found within you, in the lessons learned from your past. From the lessons passed on to you from all who *came and went before you.*

Strength is found within our creator; therefore, this strength is already present within you. As is the unconditional love, the understanding, intelligence, and joyfulness.

We love you,
The Angels

Thank you, Angels for that powerful message. To everyone reading this know you can call upon the Angels to help you in all areas of your life. The Angels come through with this message to remind us all they are already an empowered being.

I have traveled my own journey which in the end led me back to my purpose. As much as I know this message from the Angels is for all of us reading it, I cannot help but to feel humbled by it. In my life I have remained silent and tried to fit in. Tried living my life through the ideals of how others thought I should be living. This did not work for me, not in the long scheme of things.

Through the wisdom I have gained I would

advise every person in this world not to accept conditional love and acceptance. Now more than ever we need lightworkers, people dedicated to being of service. Whether you do this through mediumship or through service organizations, or by helping someone in need.

Spreading the energy of compassion and love verses hate and division will help bring you closer to the Creator and bring humanity together.

When I answered the call to be of service for the spirit world through mediumship, I did so with the intention of helping those here on earth and there in the spirit realm. Not only in providing proof of life after death, but to give people who had lost any hope of an afterlife confidence that it exists by giving spirit a voice. I wanted to open people's minds to the greatness of our creator. Wishing to reawaken those who were sleep walking through their lives.

LOVE IS WHAT MATTERS

I have never met anyone in spirit who came to me who tells their loved ones, "I wish I would have stomped on the hearts of those sensitives."

Or "I wished I would have spent less time with those I loved!" Many have regrets of the way they treated their loved ones or people while they were here. We have so much we could learn from them. All the "I love you's" left unspoken; the "I am sorry's" never said. Spirit messages to us are focused on compassion and love. Things like we want you to be happy, thank you for taking care of me, thank you for holding my hand. I love you.

THERE WERE TIMES OF CONFLICT WITHIN

There were times when I went through a period of great conflict over where my abilities stemmed from. Conflicted over whether I was good or evil. Especially when bad things started to happen to me and those I love. I let doubts and fear creep into my head instead of paying attention to what I knew inside of myself. This can be an easy trap to fall into. Life can be confusing enough without all of us seeking control over others. Especially by using fear-based information. Bullying, ostracizing or any form of rejection, or in some cases shunning - all of this may appear to work. Trust me it is just an illusion and is not the answer.

I want to state I understand the necessity of order, and its importance in society. That is not what I am referring to here. I have respect for others who have a different belief system. My upbringing was not always perfect, but it turns out it was for me. I was taught to be kind, tolerant, and love is the answer to every problem in the world. The end result was my upbringing taught me to have self-worth, to have respect for all people. My upbringing taught me one human is no better than another human. I am proud of that and have raised my children the same.

If you asked me what has been the hardest for me, I would answer the lack of respect some of us as human beings give to one another in the name of our beliefs, religion, and education, when it comes to our differences.

I will never let another person's negative action change my soul, and who I am. You see only I can do that. As one of the creator's own, just think about this, consider it. Be honest with yourself. Take some time and do a life review now if you have not already done so. Ask yourself what I can do today, right now, in this moment to become a better person. Start there, one day at a time. One person at a time.

BETTER TOMORROWS

None of us can change our past, it is just not possible. We can make better tomorrows. In my mind and in my world the answer is simply love and mutual respect. Respect for one another, treating one another as we wish to be treated. Be kind, be strong. Learn about our differences. None of us need to take on the differences as part of our own belief. What matters most is our inner goodness and how we love others while we are here. Nothing else is of value, not our status in life, our religion, our ethnicity. No one soul is better than another. Remember we are all souls, who are having a human experience. For the love of our Creator, strive to be the best human.

Heaven can be on earth. We could all learn so much from Spirit. I thank God every day for the gift of Mediumship.

My maternal grandmother taught me well many years ago.

I can still hear her beautiful, deep, soulful voice telling me that I had a little voice inside of me.

"I do?"

"Yes, you do. And if you listen to it, that little voice will never lead you wrong."

She had deep soulful eyes that twinkled as she interacted with you. "It is right here," she said pointing to my heart. When she said this to me, she used her fingertip to trace an invisible swirling line on my heart, tapping lightly, then down to my belly, where she did a swirl on my belly, then back up again.

"Do you know where the little voice is," she asked? "No," she answered for me.

"Listen, do you hear it?" she wanted to know.

Touching my heart again she said, "See? This is where the little voice is, it is right here!"

"Do not worry it is there. Be quiet and listen, do you hear it?"

Tracing an imaginary line with her finger down to my stomach. Giving me one last reminder, "Remember this little voice will never lead you wrong, so when you do not know what to do listen to it tell you. Trust it, and you will always be taken care of."

Once more she traced the imaginary line back to my heart and kissed my forehead.

The things you see when you are aware! Knowing what I know now, it makes my heart smile.

Thank you for reading my story,
Deborah

Epilogue

I would describe the field of mediumship as a calling. As a vocation, mediumship should be focused on service. Being a medium comes with a lot of responsibility. I did not choose how the Creator made me, in fact I spent a lot of years denying and fighting that part of me.

When I chose to stop living in fear-based energy and not let the opinions of others bother me that was when I was able to live the life the creator had planned for me. I finally found the key to unlocking my soul-self by surrendering. Through the surrendering, trusting in the wisdom of God, my focus became more about honoring the Creator and the way He created me, making myself available to be of service.

I work for spirit, meaning those who have crossed over, through Mediumship. I am the person who stands in between worlds, holding a conversation with those in Heaven and delivering their messages to their loved one. With my whole heart, it is my hope to provide those who are left here to mourn, a little peace and comfort. If I could be instrumental in helping in their process of grieving, I am blessed.

As I reminisce now, I can clearly see the answer to what I was shown all those years ago. As the information began to unfold before me, it was like unfolding a map and seeing how what looked to be a detour was not a detour at all. This ended up being the best route to the destination of mediumship and to mentoring others.

It all made perfect sense as to why I was called back to Mediumship and where the journey took me and why I acquired the skills I had learned during those years where I was not a psychic-medium anymore. Following the Creator's plan and my knowing helped to fulfil my role in all of it.

Using my abilities for over two and a half decades now, I have consistently witnessed Spirits ability to help provide healing within the messages to the ones who seek me out. Since it is one of my greatest desires to be able to provide a little slice of heaven's peace to their loved ones who are grieving, I am dedicated to being of service in this manner.

As much as I had wished I was not in my late twenties when I found out about my mom being gifted, I have come to understand that was all supposed to be part of my journey as well.

When I think back to the very first Spiritual Development Circle the memory makes me smile. I am so proud of these individuals. These women had put their faith and trust in me. They trusted me to lead and guide them on their journey of self-discovery or in some cases rediscovery. My thought when starting this group was to educate them, by helping them debunk fears, and superstitions and perhaps help them understand some of the things they were experiencing or had experienced.

Showing them through my own example of how not be afraid of being powerful or being true to their authentic selves. You see each of these women were psychics, and mediums. Some just had not remembered that yet and some had not ever acknowledged it. Some still study with me, others moved into the business. There are those who are constant, even when a new group comes in.

A friend and colleague had asked me to brainstorm with her one day on an idea she had. Throughout our conversation we realized all the synchronicity going on, both with our lives and with the universe.

Many of us had heard the call from the Creator God, and spirit and had been working towards living our purpose while giving others a helping hand-up.

The Universe is listening. I love the way the Universe and spirit works, don't you?

THANKS AND TESTIMONIALS FROM CLIENTS

#1

"I wanted to thank you so much for my reading. You truly have a gift! I am still blown away at the messages I received from my angels. There were a few messages that were unclear to me but then after talking to my mom and grandmother, they knew exactly what they were about! You have really helped me put a few things I was unsure of behind me. It is amazing how your angels know exactly what messages need to come through at a specific time in your life! I really cannot thank you enough!

I look forward to taking your angel card reading class and I will tell everyone I know how amazing and talented you are!" - M

#2

"Deb is a very caring and compassionate lady. She has a wonderful gift and is incredibly talented at what she does. She works hard to bring messages through clearly.

I contacted Deb as I recently lost my sweet dog

who had been part of our family for 16 years. Whilst I felt she (Cassie) was showing me signs she was still around, I needed proof this was indeed her.

Deb gave me a wonderful reading which validated Cassie is still around me. One of the signs I received was confirmed with precise detail regarding the timing.

Deb gave me details relating to Cassie's passing and health conditions prior to. Each one I could relate to. She tuned into her personality and got it exactly right.

Deb also passed on messages about other family pets plus a family member in spirit which were correct. I would recommend a reading with Deb, as mine brought great comfort to our family." – S.B.

#3

"I will never forget the first time I met Deborah Finley OMG! I was in between the sky and earth floating without any direction. It was November 2014. My cousin, who was a Shaman, had passed three days before and he was giving me instructions; messages and demands on how to carry on his work. He had been teaching me since I was seven years old. As soon as I saw Deborah's face it all made sense. She said he was sitting behind me. He started talking to her and she confirmed all he was telling me.

I had a car accident this August. Once again, she was on point with what the universe was saying. She explained it in such a way I was able to understand the process.

Deborah is just an awesome soul. Her aura engulfs yours, making you feel free to just accept and open to the real you. The feeling is phenomenal. I was never like everyone, could never fit in my thoughts and visions which meant a lot to me, until I met like-minded people. Thank you, Deborah, of all 14 past lives I remember, I could not identify with this one until I met you. I am no longer stuck between earth and sky. I can travel again." - A.

#4

"I had the most amazing reading with Deb Finley this week. She connected to current events in my life... my thoughts, hopes and dreams. She was in touch with a deceased loved one... I felt like he was right there on the phone with us. All my concerns were addressed without having to mention them. This was the most accurate and personal connection I have had. Deb is a delight! Blessings." - J.

#5

"Deborah made a believer out of me years ago. Her accuracy is spot on. Deborah has the ability to foresee the future as well as connect with those who have passed on. I have sent those I love to her for readings because of her integrity." – B

#6

"My brother died very unexpectedly and at a very young age.

There were a lot of unanswered questions.... Did he suffer, was there foul play involved? etc... I spoke with my brother through Deb for an hour. I forgot Deb was there. She spoke just like he did! All his little quirks of speech, hand gestures and slang. What a gift! I cannot thank you enough Deb for the beautiful healing your session had for me and my whole family!

FOR ME THERE IS NO DOUBT I GOT TO SPEAK TO MY BROTHER ONE LAST TIME. THANK YOU!" - AMY P.

Glossary

CAUL

A caul is a piece of membrane that can cover a newborn's face. It is considered rare. Even rarer is an en caul birth in which the baby is born still inside the amniotic sac, fully intact. It is believed that those born en caul or with a caul (veil) have psychic gifts.

CHAKRA

Translates to "wheel" or "disk". Chakra refers to wheels of energy throughout the body.

EN TRANCE

A state of half-conscious wakefulness in which the person who trances moves aside and grants spirit access to use the medium's body to give messages.

SITTER

A person who sits before the medium; one who receives a reading or message from Spirit through the medium.

CLAIR

Clairs are psychic gifts. It is the ability to read the energy of a person, place, or thing.

I.E.T.

Integrated Energy Therapy®, also known as IET® for short. IET® is often described as Healing with the energy of the Angels.

RUNES

Small stones, pieces of wood or clay

tablets, bearing a mark or letter of an ancient Germanic alphabet.

ORACLE   A term used for someone who predicts future events, the word itself comes from Latin oraculum meaning "to speak".

PERIPHERAL NERVOUS
SYSTEM   The peripheral nervous system connects the body as a whole to the central nervous system through 31 pairs of spinal nerves, which link to the spinal cord, and 12 pairs of cranial nerves, which link directly to the brain itself.

Retrieved from https://www.britannica.com/science/human-nervous-system/The-peripheral-nervous-system on 7/7/2020

QI   In Chinese culture, Qi is considered "air", "life force", or "energy flow" and is a foundational belief in traditional Chinese medicine and martial arts.

PRANA   Prana is a Sanskrit word that has many interpretations in English, which includes "life Force", "energy", and "vital principle", Prana refers to all the manifest energy in the universe, present in living beings and inanimate objects according to Hindu and yoga philosophy.

Deborah A. Finley has over two decades of experience reading for individuals professionally. She is a spiritual evidential medium, spiritual teacher, certified angel card reader, and an ordained minister. Deborah has embraced the principles of the Spiritualist religion.

She is a best-selling published author. Her story, *Surrendering to Your Divine Purpose* in the co-authored best seller book, **Women Standing Strong Together**, is where she shares the exact moment, she knew just how important her abilities were. Her channeled message from the Angels was recently published in the best-selling co-authored book, **The Path to Awakening**.

Deborah has been a natural medium all her life. Since she was a young child, she has had the ability to communicate with spiritual beings. After having a near death experience, her abilities became even more super-charged. It is her hope to provide comfort and a sense of peace to those she reads for, confirming the survival of the soul after physical death takes place.

In her free time, Deborah enjoys painting Angels, and writing. She loves spending time on the beach, with her family at the New Jersey shore, and traveling with her loved ones. She is passionate and dedicated to educating, and helping others develop and understand their gift of mediumistic abilities.

To schedule your group event or private reading email Deborah at: info@Angel-Energy.org

Visit her Website: www.Angel-Energy.org

www.PPP-Publishing.com
828-713-3521

Printed in Great Britain
by Amazon

46005261R00139